THE AIM OF THIS BOOK is
producing books that will
public libraries, or marketed on the internet.

A glossary of terms is used, not for word definitions, but to give ideas and solutions for the range of processes you need as a small publisher. It is intended to be thought-provoking and to save some of the mistakes in DIY publishing, especially in relation to timing the publishing process. This is so important that a timing guide is presented as an appendix.

A glossary is in itself a word list, but a simple index is included to help readers follow the main processes of publishing a book. For example, 'marketing' directs the reader to pages where references to marketing occur.

There is no bibliography because *Bring It to Book* is derived from the author's personal experience, printing short-run books for hundreds of small publishers since 1987. A list of helpful reference books is included instead.

It is not within the book's compass to give advice about different computer systems and wordprocessing software. PC people and Mac people are coming closer together, and there are many books covering these subjects readily available.

By the same author:

Echoes From The Land (Scriptmate Editions, London 1996)

20,000 Leagues Under The Sea (New English Library, London 1978)

Alice in Wonderland (New English Library, London 1978)

The Strongest Man in the World (New English Library, London 1976)

Superdad (New English Library, London 1976)

Darby O'Gill and The Little People (New English Library, London 1976)

Lib & Let Lib (Roger Schlesinger, London 1975)

'Blood on the Mountain', *Memorable School Stores* anthology (Octopus Books, London 1980)

New English Library publications adapted from Walt Disney Productions' screen presentations under the pseudonym Ann Spano

ANN KRITZINGER

*Bring It
To Book*

STEPS TO SUCCESS FOR SMALL PUBLISHERS

SCRIPTMATE EDITIONS 1997

First published in 1997
by Scriptmate Editions
20 Shepherds Hill,
London N6 5AH

© 1997 Ann Kritzinger
Cover cartoon copyright © 1997 A Krauze

ISBN 0-9513766-8-3

A CIP record for this book is available from the British Library

Distributed by Vine House Distribution
Tel 01825 723398/fax 01825 724188

Ann Kritzinger's right to be identified as the author of this work has been asserted by her in accordance with the Copyright, Designs and Patents Act 1988.

All rights reserved. No part of this book may be reproduced by any means, electronic or mechanical, including photocopy or any information storage and retrieval system without permission in writing from the publisher.

While every effort has been made to trace copyright holders and obtain permission, this has not been possible in all cases. Any omissions brought to our attention will be remedied in future editions.

Typeset in New Century 11/13pt
Manufacture coordinated
by Book-in-Hand Ltd
London N6 5AH

Dedicated to

Giles Taylor for his many hours keying in
draft corrections and handwritten additions

Sara Peacock for copy editing and
professional finesse

gremlin errors 'let go'

Contents

INTRODUCTION	9
GLOSSARY	13
STEP-BY-STEP CHECKLIST	141
FURTHER READING	143
INDEX	145

Book-in-Hand Ltd regrets that Scriptmate Editions cannot accept unsolicited submissions

We are happy to receive letters from readers, or specifications for estimates, but if you would like Ann Kritzinger to answer any specific queries, please enclose £2 per question with an sae to: Dept B2, Booksend, Freepost, London N6 5BR

Introduction
with special reference to self-publishing

To launch into a market that is made up of 100,000 different product lines in the UK alone is not easy.

Spectacular successes are rare, yet we've all heard about the go-it-alone enterprises in 1995 of Timothy Mo, Jill Paton-Walsh and Helen McCabe, one of my own customers. Another successful customer is VJ Hewitt whose self-published *Nostradamus Understood* was found in a library by a packager's secretary in 1990. A coffee table edition was published by Bloomsbury and Simon & Schuster in 1991. To date over a million hardbacks have been sold in four translations. The author now has an agent, with other titles commissioned by Reed International Books and Random House.

Self-publishing is not new. It has its roots in social protest and freedom of speech. Socrates was a self-publisher. In the Middle Ages—and in some countries to the present day—'unlicensed printing' risked punishment, even death.

Robinson Crusoe is acclaimed as the first English novel but it was published by an obscure printer for Daniel Defoe after blanket rejection by publishing houses in Britain. Conrad published his first novel. Tolstoy paid $12,700 to publish *War and Peace*. *Tarzan* was self-published by Edgar Rice Burroughs. Marcel Proust, unable to find a publisher for *Remembrance of Things Past*, paid for the publication of the first 1,500 pages in France. As did the modern best-selling poet Rod McKuen, who published his first book in the US himself. Booker author Roddy Doyle revealed on national TV that he self-published his first book.

Publishers' print runs have reduced significantly over the

last decade, especially for books by first-time authors. So it is easier for small and self-publishers to become players in the marketplace. Self-publishers can sell over a thousand copies if the package is right, but it is best to be realistic about sales potential until the unexpected happens. Don't expect a publisher to 'take you up'—they tend to view previously published titles as 'secondhand goods', especially in the UK. Booksellers, with their premium on shelf space, are wary about one-offs.

Many writers have told me that self-publishing is fun, even that it has given them a new lease of life in advancing age. My oldest customer is in his nineties and has ceased publishing new titles only because he doesn't want to outstrip Moses, 'who stopped at four'. Recently the BBC filmed his short boyhood autobiography.

A film is to be made of Chili Bouchier's *Shooting Star—Last of the Silent Film Stars*. She published the hardback edition herself at eighty-six and Scriptmate Editions published a paperback edition for her while she reprinted. She is now represented by a distinguished literary agent. She is a star in so many ways that no apology is needed for her strong presence in these pages. It also allows a glimpse at one title's success.

Three more of my customers have had films made of their books, another three are on option. Large print and talking book rights can be negotiated.

Going it alone seems to be more acceptable since the fall of the Net Book Agreement, particularly now that corporate publishing houses, which swallowed up the independents in recent decades, are giving as much attention to their account books as to their commissioned books. There is nothing wrong in this—it is healthy market practice—but it narrows the field of selection, squeezing out 'high risk' new writers and established writers who have not kept up with changing demands and styles.

A big difference between publishers and self-publishers

is the strength of attachment they have for their products. Publishers know that printers treat each title as work-in-progress. But self-publishers are often producing a life work, bringing a dream to reality. They assume their words are lovingly read by typesetters and printers, their pictures known by the precise image and the exact position in the text, their page running order apparent although their camera-ready copy is not numbered. This is delusion. Printers treat words, images and pagination as technicalities. Booksellers often ignore them, but if they are well presented and the cover is good they might make a purchase.

*

Most successful books have had some professional design or editorial guidance, in my experience.

Time and care spent before publication are never wasted. Snippets of advice are:

Get all the professional editing help you can with fiction.

Make exhaustive double checks with non-fiction.

Cut autobiographies to local interest episodes for slim volumes if you can't afford to print 400-pagers—and they will be much easier to sell.

Don't print a large number of copies because of a hypothetical net profit you can make. Tailor your dream book to what you can afford and price it at what the market can stand. If it sells at this level, you can embark upon a longer print run which might make you a modest profit.

A secret of success with self-publishing is to familiarise yourself with as many of the publishing processes as possible. If you are going to do your own origination on a desktop system, then you should at least take a book on typography out of the library. Notice how prelims or appendices run in a conventional book. Note how dialogue is punctuated, how indexes and bibliographies are laid out.

Carefully plan the final size of your book, and allow camera-ready text to have adequate margins. Take care that copyright is cleared for pictures and the work is carefully copy-edited.

Get the total package right and you stand to make more than the 7–10 per cent author's royalties you could expect if you were fortunate enough to be accepted by a publishing house. It is a hard road but it can be taken successfully with a lot of planning, leg work and a little luck.

A

A-SIZES Modular sizes based on a rectangle with the area of 1 sq metre. A1 = 841 x 594mm, A2 = 594 x 420mm, A3 = 420 x 297mm, A4 = 297 x 210mm, A5 = 148 x 210m.

Think carefully about A-size default formats on computer systems. They can be printers' nightmares because they seldom give enough margin allowance for guillotine trim at binding. It is always better to design books in sizes traditional to the publishing world. (See Format.)

ACCENTS Use sparingly and not for common words such as 'role', 'fete', or 'cafe'. If your system's accents don't translate into typesetters' systems (Amstrad incompatibility for instance), accent codes can be keyed into your word processor in ASCII key strokes. The international character set code for 'e acute' is <130> (é); for 'o circumflex' it is <147> (ô). Full lists of codes are available—a few fonts use different codes (e.g. <165> and <162> for the accents above).

A mathematical genius in Denmark spent days working out a system of ASCII codes, up to twelve letters long, which he was convinced would accent his Czechoslovakian travel guide correctly. Not only had every one to be stripped out manually, but his text files were excessively large, incurring extra cost at conversion stage.

It is often easier to mark up accents at proof stage.

ACCOUNTANT It is advisable to seek the advice of an accountant if your book begins to sell, or if you are taking up self-publishing for more than one title.

ACCOUNTING Keep a simple profit and loss account and copies of all invoices. Against sales can come items like post and packing materials and cost of delivery from the printer or binder. Set these against profit when that time comes.

ACKNOWLEDGEMENTS Keep your list under control and your thanks expressed professionally. Think of a way you can thank your partner other than 'last but not least for his/her patience and understanding'.

ADJECTIVES Try not to use more than two adjectives to a noun, especially when describing inanimate household objects (contemporary characters in a historical novel would not think of a chair in terms of its highly polished cabriole legs). In non-fiction 'a bird in the bush' communicates more directly than 'a feathered friend in the verdant undergrowth'.

ADVANCE INFORMATION Crucial for successful publishing, this is information about your title which should be mailed to prospective sales' outlets at least three months before publication date (not to be confused with delivery-from-the-printer date). It should include details about your title, in addition to 'selling copy' (see Blurb) and a piece about the author (see Biog). It can also include a picture of the front cover and a sales coupon. Returning the Whitaker book information form completed as early as possible is important advance information too.

ADVERBS Hyphenate only if describing nouns, for instance 'a well-baked cake', but use no hyphen if 'the cake was well baked'. The many English words ending in 'ly' are not hyphenated: 'lightly frosted icing'.

ADVERTISING A costly way of publicising your book but essential to launch 'bestsellers'. If you are selling by direct mail, small ads placed in suitable media can be very worthwhile. To record responss, code each insertion 'Dept WM' for *Writing Magazine* or 'Dept RM' for a regimental magazine.

Vine House Distribution

Waldenbury, North Common, Chailey,
East Sussex BN8 4DR, England
Tel: 01825-723398
Fax: 01825-724188

ADVANCE INFORMATION SHEET

TITLE:	SHOOTING STAR : THE LAST OF THE SILENT FILM STARS
ISBN:	0 9526488 0 6 HB PRICE: £14.99
	0 9513766 6 7 PB PRICE: £ 8.99
AUTHOR:	Chili Bouchier PUBLISHER: Atlantis / Scriptmate Editions
PUBLICATION DATE:	January/February 1996 CATEGORY: Biography/Cinema
SPECIFICATIONS:	HB/PB 248 pages 217 x 140mm 81 b/w photographs
	3 colour cover highlighted by silver foil

DESCRIPTION: One of the grand old girls of British Cinema has committed her life to print. Chili Bouchier, 86, is about to launch her memoirs, **Shooting Star**.

For the cover Miss Bouchier has chosen a bare-chested pose of herself from her 1931 film 'Carnival'. So risque was the photograph considered at the time that newspapers refused to print it. The contents are equally hot. Miss Bouchier, once the country's sex symbol, thrice turned down proposals for marriage from the American billionaire Howard Hughes.

Another financier, John Paul Getty, has helped fund the book, with a birthday present to Miss Bouchier of £5,000.

Chili Bouchier was born in London in 1909. She entered films in 1927 at the age of seventeen and within a year became England's first sex symbol - known as Britain's 'IT' Girl and Britain's Clara Bow. Chili made a successful transition into Talkies in 1929. She has been part of the movie and theatre scene for nearly seventy years and is the last surviving star of the Silent Screen.

Chili calls her book **Shooting Star** because, she says, there were times when she shone brilliantly and others when she almost disappeared from view. Her book is not a typical show-biz autobiography but the true story of a woman's life with its ups and downs, triumphs and failures, joys and sorrows - and some paranormal experiences.

PUBLICITY: 'Shooting Star' has been widely featured in the national press and on radio and TV. Extensive further coverage is assured throughout January and February.

DISTRIBUTION: Vine House Distribution (details as above)

Warehousing · Distribution Worldwide · Representation · Order Processing · Cash Collection
Publicity & Promotion · Press & Public Relations · Mail Order · Exhibitions · Book Trade Mailings

Advance information is extremely important in the publishing process. This is the distributor's AI for Chili Bouchier's *Shooting Star*

ALCS Authors' Licensing & Collecting Society. A company limited by guarantee (i.e. not having a share capital) run by members through a council of management. It keeps a watching brief on, and is a collective administration for, all copyright matters affecting the UK and other countries. It has a definitive role in setting copyright parameters for electronic publishing for the new millennium.

AMPERSAND The shortened form of 'and'. Use it sparingly, even in headlines. Don't use it in proof corrections, assuming the typesetter will know you really mean 'and'.

ANACHRONISM In writing terms this is a character in an 18th-century novel, say, who speaks and behaves in a 20th-century manner.

ANGLE Better than advertisements are editorial mentions gained from a good press release. But a press release will only work if it has an angle—a hook to hang a story on. Like a Chelsea Pensioner who sold out his self-published autobiography at the Chelsea Flower Show after his press release announced they were both seventy-five that year.

APOSTROPHE Don't abuse this little mark, especially if you are producing camera-ready copy. Professional typesetting does not permit an apostrophe used in the wrong place.

Don't use an apostrophe indiscriminately before an 's' whether plural or not. When not used to indicate a possessive it replaces a missing letter, for instance, let's (short for 'let us') not lets; '30s (not 30's). Regarding dates, 1900s not 1900's is correct.

'It's/its' is often maligned. 'It's' is correct when it means 'it is'. When it's possessive use 'its'—'its time is up', like 'his (or her) time is up'.

For single open quotation marks printing as apostrophes, see Smart Key.

APPENDIX Additional information which follows the main

body of text. Make sure appendices add value and are not too long. Self-publishers often include material which is important to themselves but is meaningless to others, such as the surgeon who copied all the medical appointment letters in his long career, increasing the book (and the cost) by 20 per cent, and the many self-publishers who want to include press cuttings about themselves in their entirety (reduced to an unreadable size).

ARABIC NUMBERS Use these wherever possible, especially for chapter numbers and dates. It is better to leave prelim pages unnumbered before the body of the book starts with the relevant arabic number ('9' as in this book). If you start the main body of the book at '1' remember to include the number of prelim pages for any information regarding the extent of the book, especially for a printer's estimate.

ARCHIVE Computer-speak for 'save'. If your book is digitally printed, make sure it is saved for reprints (you may be asked to pay a small fee). With digital printing there is no film (or plates) and, if it is not archived—having no 'standing matter', your book can disappear into the ether. .

ART The term for hard copy illustration, etc., hence 'artwork'. Don't expect a printer to make a professional cover or jacket from your rough. You will need to provide good quality originals and a clearly indicated position guide. Many printers only accept camera-ready artwork or PostScript print files ready for printing.

ART PAPER Clay-coated paper with a glossy surface.

ARTICLE Be discriminating with 'the' 'a' or 'an'. The replacement of one for another (or its elimination) can change the emphasis of a sentence.

An article can also be a piece about you or your book in a newspaper or journal—if you're lucky enough to get one.

ARTIST You should respect artists' work by paying an adequate fee. You should acknowledge that copyright is theirs unless you pay an agreed fee over and above the execution fee. It is a good idea to brief an artist to design your cover. If an illustrator is acknowledged on the title page, s/he is entitled to a share of public lending right payment.

AS A word too liberally used. Try 'while', 'because', 'since', 'during'. Or, better still, rephrase the sentence.

ASCII Text with no embedded processing or print information. Such a file can be read into many systems and is sometimes asked for by printers and typesetters. (ASCII stands for 'American Standard Code For Information Interchange. Desktop people will eschew ASCII, but it is professionally used by typesetters).

AUTHOR The creator who should take a back seat in the publishing process when s/he is the publisher. This is because authors are too close to their work and necessary contingency measures (such as cutting text or discarding pictures) are likely to be taken too personally for the good of the product or, ultimately, the budget.

AUTHOR'S CORRECTIONS All corrections you make on proofs received from the printer, typesetter or desktop bureau, other than any originated by them. The cost of author's corrections is high, yet self-publishers are constantly rewriting their books at proof stage. Professional publishers protect themselves by committing their authors to the cost of corrections in excess of 10 per cent of the original cost of composition. Self-publishers have to pay the whole bill.

Use one ballpoint colour for your errors and another for any printers' errors. It is safer and cheaper to have the work at final finished stage before sending it to a printer or typesetter.

---G

GALLEY PROOF The text of a book in a continuous column, without page breaks. This was the way proofs were set before the age of computer page make-up systems, and desktop publishing which goes straight to page.

GATHER Assembly of collated sheets, or folded sections of a book before binding. [stet]

GHOST An unnamed writer who composes someone else's /idea or story into words.

GLOSSARY Definitions in alphabetical order. Often used to explain foreign words/phrases or technical terms. You shouldn't find it necessary to explain generally used words [commonly] or items especially in works of fiction.

GLUE-BINDING Glue-binding has improved for paperbacks in the last decade. Slimmer copies are cheaper to bind because they require less glue and fewer boxes for packing. The longer the print run, the stronger the binding and the lower the unit cost.

GRAIN The direction in which the fibres of paper or board run. Long grain runs parallel to the long edge of the paper. For best results pages and covers should be printed with the grain running lengthwise. Otherwise covers won't lie flat and pages will curl or buckle'. Many digital printers print two-to-view books on the short grain. Their books could be improved if they bound on the outside edge, not centrally. There are ways to achieve this very easily.

GRAMMAR Good grammar means easier communication. Take control of your sentences. Shorten them and construct them well to express yourself with clarity. [new para] [this]

GRAMMAGE Weight of stock (paper or card).

44

---

non-fiction. It is particularly valuable for keeping abreast of changing styles in your chosen genre.

MARKETING Marketing is a crucial part of commercial self-publishing. It's no use treating it as an afterthought. It should be planned, budgeted for and initiated long before publication date. It starts with planning—including preparation and/or purchase of mailing lists—continues through well-timed advance information and media bookproofs for review, to author talks or signing sessions after publication. It also means cold calling, featuring in exhibitions and trying for subsidiary rights sales.

Learn as much as possible about your market and take every step to make sure it knows about you and your title. Knowing your non-fiction public is a good starting place. Make a comprehensive but selective media list for review copies. Even self-publishers of fiction can be well reviewed if targeting and timing is planned ahead. Enter competitions [are] open to published work, except where self-published titles are specifically barred.

The cover is crucial packaging. Get it wrong and nobody is going to find out what goes on inside the book. Many booksellers won't purchase books with imprints they don't know.

MARK UP Copy marked with information for the typesetter or printer. In professional publishing this is a skilled job requiring knowledge of typography, layout, style, and design. (z)

Freelance copy editors expect £11/15 an hour. The very minimum you should present to your typesetter or printer is a style sample (a page or two from a book you like for instance). Indicate any subhead changes (Head1, Head2, etc.), rather than expect the typesetter to spot any slight difference in weight, position or spacing from your typewriter or desktop printer. [?]

Only copy submitted camera-ready will not require mark-up or design instructions, whether this be hardcopy or

62

Printer's proofs should be marked with essential corrections only. On the left, the author's amendments; on the right, the final copy edit. There were many wordprocessor drafts of this book, but if proofs are treated as working drafts, the cost will be very high

19

Any errors in copy submitted on disk are yours as the originator. They will be charged for, as will errors missed on the first proof but spotted in a subsequent one, even if they were originally 'printer's errors'. The standard conditions of the printing industry are:

> The printer shall incur no liability for any errors not corrected by the customer in proofs. Customer's alterations and additional proofs necessitated thereby shall be charged extra. When style, type or layout is left to the printer's judgement, changes therefrom made by the customer shall be charged extra.

Take care that your correction marks can be clearly understood. Scrambled, illegible corrections will cost you more in deciphering time. If you decide to use capital letters for legibility (not the best idea), make sure you indicate those letters that are to be set in caps.

AUTOBIOGRAPHY A category that can have a valuable social comment to make. But it is invariably too long and often self-indulgent in terms of content and illustrations. If the author is not well known this category is very difficult to sell. Set your sights lower—autobiographers can be successful if their work has a local slant.

B

BACKLIST Previously published titles—a valuable publisher resource. This doesn't mean booksellers will warehouse these books, but that their names are held on a database.

As a self-publisher, you can keep your title in print for as long as you can sell it. You must store copies in a dry place, pack and dispatch them, invoice correctly and promote them regularly.

BACKGROUND In-depth information in fiction and non-fiction. Used in production terms, it generally means tint or colour enhancing to the main image. It can be used extremely effectively in cover design.

BACKING UP (COMPUTER) Get into the habit of saving your work onto floppy disk, especially at the day's end. Use good quality disks. 'Unknown Error' is too depressing a message when you need to load a disk after a period of time.

BACKING UP (PRINTER) The printing of lines of text or images on one side of a page lining up with those on the other side. Hold proof pages to the light and check page numbers against each other. They should be spot on for offset litho and not more than 1mm out in digital print.

BANK ACCOUNT There is no need to open a separate bank account, unless your book is going to sell over 1000 copies, when it will be easier for accounting purposes. Be careful not to go into the red if you open a business account which has heavier penalties than a private account.

BAR CODE If you are targeting libraries or larger booksellers a bar code is useful. It should be placed bottom right, on the back cover. (A simple bar code does not include price.) Some colours will be readable (for instance this book's bar code could have been printed blue or green on yellow) but it is safest to stick to black for printing the bar code. If you slip up, quality bar code labels are acceptable.

BESTSELLER No harm in hoping for a bestseller but the statistical likelihood is that your book won't make it. If your title does top the charts, the volume of sales will be too great for you to handle without professional help.

BIBLIOGRAPHY List of sources used in producing the text. Don't neglect to include a list of reference books in your non-fiction book. It should contain details of publisher as well as title and author. Check through your bookshelf to see ways in which bibliographies can be laid out.

BINDING Forget about a dream baby cased in tooled leather! The decision whether to publish in hardback or in paperback is very difficult. Self-publishers can make more profit on the cover price of hardbacks than the extra it costs to bind them. But booksellers and libraries are swinging heavily in favour of paperbacks. There are exceptions of course, particularly children's, cookery and reference books. Large print books used to be exclusively thread sewn hardbacks until the recent discovery that elderly people preferred something less weighty to read in bed.

One solution is to run a paperback edition with a shorter run of hardbacks. With careful planning, origination cost can be little more than the amount for one edition.

BIOG Biographical note on the back cover, also included in advance information. Keep it very short. Restrict it to details relevant to your subject matter. Any track record is important, even for fiction—having been a barrister, say, adds authenticity to a crime novel. Don't include very minor educational achievements, nor phrases such as 'likes to be creative'.

BIT The computer unit 1 or 0.

BLACK In printing terms black is a colour. A two-colour cover can be red and black, or yellow and blue like this cover.

BLEED Amount of extra image required to allow a picture and/or background colour to extend beyond the image area of a page, cover or jacket. It should be generous enough to allow for trim, approx 4–10mm.

BLOCK (MENTAL) The best antidote is setting words down on paper—any words. Leave work in mid-sentence to allow easy pick-up next time. Be disciplined and professional rather than 'creative'.

BLOCK (METAL) The stamp for impressing, for example, in foil on a cover. When used 'blind' it will raise or depress the image.

BLOW UP Enlarge, particularly in respect of pictures.

BLURB A descriptive passage about the book. This 'selling copy' needs to be read at a glance by punters in a bookshop, so keep it short and snappy. There is a vogue for quoting a passage from the book on the back cover or the jacket. Self-publishers need to be bolder than this. After several drafts give the copy to a professional friend to gauge if your message is coming across strongly enough. Good biogs and blurbs should be prepared early for use in advance publicity.

BOARD The correct name for card.

BOARDS The front and back stiffener to which the casing cloth is adhered for hardbacks. Its weight is usually expressed in 'sheets' i.e. '2-sheet or 3-sheet board'.

BODY COPY The main body of text of a work.

BOLD Type that is heavier than the regular or normal typeface used. You might find some bold in non-fiction (especially training manuals), but good quality fiction seldom has any 'bold face'.

BOOK AID INTERNATIONAL A registered charity which sends donated books to schools, colleges, universities and libraries in developing countries. If they take your remainders, it is a better solution than pulping them.

BOOK BLOCK Loose, sewn or glued pages of a book before it is bound into its cover.

BOOK CLUB It is very unlikely that large book clubs will take on your title. Only mass-market selling can give profits over and above the discounts they offer and it is unlikely you could finance the necessary print run. Some book clubs print their own edition and this is a better option. There's no harm in trying if you are convinced your book is outstanding in its category.

BOOK PROOF/SALES PROOF Large publishers have a very short run of uncorrected proof copies to use for 'taster' and review copies. It would be non-productive to send a proof that hasn't been thoroughly corrected as a small publisher. But you can use a digital printer to run 30–100 copies of your final product to use in this way. (See Taster Copies.)

BOOKSELLER There are many types of bookseller, from well-known chains to small independents. They have different procedures for purchasing but there is nothing to stop you asking managers if you can show them a copy of your book. Handling many small accounts is cost- and time-consuming, so booksellers' customers enquiring after self-published titles can be turned away with, 'we don't stock it'. Independent booksellers are more accommodating to their customers—they know that single self-published orders won't carry a surcharge and that they are likely to receive that order by return.

Some bookseller chains find it too time-consuming to set up an account for yet another publisher, especially one with only one title to offer. Others base orders on the amount of money invested in promotion. The more zeros the larger the order. (Overheard at John Menzies, 'if the print run is 25,000, we expect a £25,000 promotional budget.') Chains' individual stores can often purchase direct, but be prepared for returns.

BOOKSHOP You must be able to walk into a bookshop and sell your own title. In the UK there is one bookshop for every 7,500 people. In the US, although the market is five times larger, there is only one bookshop for every 20,000 people. But the buying threshold is much wider, with a strong accent on mail order, direct marketing and the Internet.

Take heart that many titles are purchased in twos or threes, and every bookseller reacts differently. With your rep hat on, keep your sales pitch to the manager or fiction/non-fiction purchaser short and businesslike. Take a simple order or invoice book (available from any stationers) and don't be put off by rejection. There is no telling which bookshop might take five copies, which not a single copy. If you have a professional product you will almost certainly find booksellers to stock it. But repeated rejection should indicate that yours is not a product retailers are willing to give valuable shelf room.

BOOK STALL Don't dismiss the thought of taking a stall at local fairs to sell your book. One novelist sells thousands of copies a year this way and specialist fairs can be excellent point-of-sale venues for non-fiction books.

BOOKWOVE Paper commonly used for book printing. It bulks up well, gives a value for money look allowing for a higher cover price.

BORDER Decorative box or rule, sometimes used on title pages.

BOX Ruled frame around text or pictures.

BRACKETS Brackets need punctuation attention. If the bracketed information comes within a sentence, punctuation is positioned after the close bracket. If it stands alone, the punctuation comes within it. Try not to make bracketed comments in fiction dialogue.

BRASS see Block (metal).

BREAK Space in text.

BRITISH LIBRARY Make sure you deposit one copy with The British Library, Legal Deposit Office, a national archive and the main copyright library requiring one copy of every edition published, within one month of publication. All publications are catalogued and made permanently available to the public. Many publications will be listed in the weekly *British National Bibliography*.

BROMIDE Photographic print of a black-and-white original (see PMT).

BSI 5261 British Standard Institution for copy preparation and proof correction. If you find the old copy correction marks simpler, most printers will still accept them.

BUDGET Unless you write specialist non-fiction and can command a high cover price, you are unlikely to break even on your first print run as a self-publisher. Yet you must be prepared to invest in a professional-looking product which will attract attention in over-subscribed sectors, although you should be aware that most self-published books sell slowly.

Divide your budget into four main headings:

Promotion, Origination, Production, Distribution.

If your first print run is 500 copies you can allocate £200 to spend in column 1. If it is 1000 copies and you can't spend £1000 on promotion, you can reduce the amount as shown in the example.

The hypothetical book in the example below has pictures and complicated typesetting so origination costs £1500 before a single copy is printed. Show printing and binding costs under 'production'. Distribution costs remain more or less static unless you have a lucky break with a bulk order.

RUN	1000	500
PROMOTION	£200	£200
ORIGINATION	£1500	£1500
PRODUCTION	£2200	£1250
TOTAL	£3900	£2950

SALES =	£2400	£2400
(400 copies less 40% distribution/ trade discount)		
LOSS	-£1500	-£550

Note the increasing profit the longer the print run. But look at it again with a contingency eye. If you are able to sell 400 copies of this particular book you will lose £550 with a run of 500 copies and £1500 with a run of 1000. It is best to print a small quantity of 'taster copies' first so that the capital invested is less and there are no books to remainder. You'll have a better idea of your book's market potential and won't contribute to global paper wastage, as you would if you're too optimistic too soon.

Setting a budget at an early stage will give you a framework when it comes to the tricky practicalities of origination and production. Cut a blockbuster of 500 pages to a more affordable extent when you see the printer's estimate for instance.

Don't forget to allow a contingency for VAT if typesetting is placed anywhere other than with your book printer.

BUREAUX Self-publishing is a growth market. It has fuelled a support industry of origination, production and marketing services. Some are helpful, others are self-interested. Their charges are usually high—considering many don't know too much about book production and have to farm out some of their services. Shop around is the best advice and ask to see samples of work.

BUSINESS You don't need to register as a small business but treat everything as if you are one. When you expand you will certainly need a good accountant.

BY The use of this word on jackets or covers is obsolete and indicates an amateur production.

BYTE An aggregate of bits which represents a number in computer technology.

C

CAMERA-READY COPY (CRC) Matter that requires no further work before printing. These days there may not be a photographic process involved, but the term is still used to mean 'ready to print'. It can apply to text, pictures, cover artwork, etc. If you are sending camera-ready copy to a printer it will be printed exactly as you send it.

Printers very seldom proof camera-ready copy or data submitted on disk—so make sure you ask for proofs if you need them, although you may be obliged to pay extra. For other types of origination you should get proofs automatically.

CAPTIONS Plan a systematic and easily followed system for captioning your illustrations. Printers have hundreds of pictures to position correctly and cannot be expected to follow casual instructions such as 'see page 16' remarks within your text. The best way to caption is a separate text printout (not handwritten), using code numbers related to the page numbers pictures fall on, for example, 16A and 16B (see Pictures).

If you want to caption the picture itself, use Post-it notes, adhesive labels or write in soft pencil on the back. Never caption in felt tip or ballpoint. The former can transfer to the next picture in a pile and the latter can press through to the face of the picture itself. If you move a picture in a proof don't expect the printer to alter its figure number (if it has one) or its position and page number in any list of illustrations. You must do this yourself.

CARD see Board.

CARTONS Your books will be delivered in sturdy cartons. Preferably leave the quantity in each to the printer or binder.

CASED Hardback binding—the leaves can be thread sewn (not stitched, a term for wire stapling) or glued. The former is the best but more expensive.

CASING CLOTH The covering over the boards of a hardback. Ask if the binder has any offcuts for a short run at a good price. Otherwise you will be supplied with synthetic material such as Linson—perfectly adequate if not compared with 'real' cloth.

CASTING-OFF Working out how many pages a book will make in a specified typeface (see Word Count). But it is easier to use the word count in your wordprocessor and divide by 350–500 words depending upon the page and font size you want. Fewer words for Large Print and children's books.

CATALOGUE Publisher's lists of titles can often end up unread in booksellers' storerooms. The trade is reviewing the high cost to publishers for inclusion in retailers' catalogues, and the degree of motivation from consumer catalogues.

CATALOGUING-IN-PUBLICATION (CIP) PROGRAMME The CIP Program-me is a facility to promote titles in advance of publication through the British Library's printed, CD and on-line products. These products have worldwide exposure and are used by librarians and booksellers to select titles in advance of publication. To contribute to this free service, publishers should submit advance information sheets or apply for pre-printed forms to Bibliographic Data Services Limited (BDS Ltd, 24 Nith Place, Dumfries DG1 2PN).

CATEGORY Booksellers sell in categories as much as publishers publish in them. As most authors know, books can be rejected—by publishers and by retailers—because they don't fall into a specific category. 'Crime' is a different category

Whitaker Classifications

Agriculture
Air Transport
Aircraft (Civil)
Aircraft (Military)
Anthropology
Antique Furniture
Archaeology
Architecture & Town Planning
Art, General
Art (Ceramics)
Art (Drawing & Painting)
Art (Sculpture)
Astronomy
Atlases & Maps
Bibliographies
Biography (Autobiography)
Biography (Biography)
Biology
Botany
Building
Careers
Chemistry
Children's Books
Cinema & Television
Communication Services
Computer Games
Computers, General
Computers (Hardware)
Computers (Software)
Costume
Criminology
Customs & Folklore
Dentistry
Economics
Education
Engineering, General
Engineering (Civil)
Engineering (Electrical)
Engineering (Electronic)
Entertainment
Fiction, General
Fiction, Historical
Fiction, Mystery
Fiction, Romance
Fiction, Science Fiction
Fiction, Short Stories
Fiction, War
Fiction, Western
Fishing & Hunting
Food & Drink
Forestry
Gardening
Genealogy
General Knowledge
Geography
Geology & Palaeontology
Handicrafts & Printmaking
Health & Hygiene
History, General
History (Ancient)
History (First World War)
History (Second World War)
History (Africa)
History (Asia)
History (Australasia)
History (Europe)
History (Great Britain & Ireland)
History (North America)
History (South & Central America)
Household Management
Humour
Indoor Games
Industrial Chemistry
Language
Law
Library Science & Publishing
Literature
Management & Business Administration
Mathematics
Medicine
Meteorology
Military Science
Music
Numismatics
Nursing
Occult
Pets
Philosophy
Photography
Physics
Plays
Poetry
Political Science
Psychiatry
Psychology
Public Administration
Railways
Religion
Road Transport
Road Vehicles (Civil)
Road Vehicles (Military)
School Textbooks
Science, General
Shipping & Inland Waterways
Ships (Civil)
Ships (Military)
Social Sciences
Social Welfare
Soil & Crop Science
Sport, General
Sport (Athletics)
Sport (Combat Sports)
Sport (Cricket)
Sport (Motor Sports)
Sport (Riding)
Sport (Rugby)
Sport (Soccer)
Sport (Tennis)
Stamps & Stamp Collecting
Stockbreeding & Veterinary Science
Technology & Manufacturing
Theatre
Trade & Commerce
Transport, General
Travel, General
Travel (Africa)
Travel (Asia)
Travel (Australasia)
Travel (Europe)
Travel (Great Britain & Ireland)
Travel (North America)
Travel (South & Central America)
Travel Accommodation
Zoology, General
Zoology (Birds)
Zoology (Fishes)
Zoology (Insects)
Zoology (Mammals)
Zoology (Reptiles & Amphibians)

Books sell in categories. This is a list of Whitaker categories

to 'Thriller'. Whitaker asks publishers to give an indication of subject category to assist them with correct classification. Classification on the Internet includes key words for webcrawlers.

CD-ROM Large-capacity vehicle for storing information that can be read in a display: akin to a book, but with the additional dimensions of moving images and sound. The chance for interactive participation by the reader is an exciting option for the future.

CENTRESPREAD Usually a picture section running across two pages in the middle of a book.

CHAPTER Try to keep chapters roughly even in length, neither too short nor too long.

CHARACTERS (HUMAN) In fiction your characters should live on the page through the way they act, react, talk and think. Don't introduce too many characters at once unless you really know how to handle them, especially in the first few pages—or your reader will feel the way it does when you are introduced to all the guests on arrival at a party.

CHARACTERS (PRINTING) Individual letters, figures, punctuation marks, etc. (See Word Count.)

CHROMAPRINT Type of colour proof.

CLICHE Phrases used too often soon become clichés. Use different ways to express 'he froze', 'her blood ran cold', 'a wall of silence'. Clichés are received style. Be original.

COATED PAPER Paper with a chalk coating that is used for good quality printing because it gives a sharp image. It is expensive and doesn't bulk up as well as bookwove.

CODES Computer information to print system-dedicated commands, or international ASCII keystokes for e.g. accents.

COLLABORATION Always acknowledge collaborators and give copyright permissions in the imprint page.

COLLAGE Manual or computer cut-and-paste to create an illustration. Collages can be effective and economic for cover designs (see page 37).

COLLATE Bringing together printed sections of a book. In new digital printing this stage is achieved at the same time as the pages are being printed.

COLOPHON see Imprint/logo.

COLOUR Any colour of ink (or toner) on paper is a colour, including black. Thus a two-colour cover could be red and black, or green and black, printed on white card (which is not counted as a colour). Two colours can be overprinted to achieve a third (like this book's cover which is printed blue and yellow to achieve green where they overlap), but consult your printer first. White is normally areas of paper or board left blank, except in screen process printing.

To get full-colour effects the printer uses four-colour process. These process colours —black, magenta, cyan and yellow—reproduce the multicolour effects from colour prints, transparencies or scanned images.

Solid colours cannot be printed successfully on small machines. They are best printed on larger machines—at greater cost to you. A designer for one of the major university presses wanted books printed and bound within four days. The cover artwork included two large areas of solid colour requiring extra drying time before title and author's name— left off the camera-ready copy in the rush—had to be embossed down the spine, with more drying time required before laminating. The bad planning meant he could not meet his deadline.

Solid colours can set off from one printed cover to another, so allow extra copies to allow for discarding spoils. With new digital technology four-colour covers can cost less than three-colour ones.

COMMAS There is a vogue to use commas 'where you would breathe'. Pointing out to a customer that her sentences needed restructuring for the meaning to be communicated more precisely without her plethora of commas, she explained that she suffered from asthma. Professionally, commas are sparingly used these days. A well-constructed sentence should not need to be heavily punctuated.

COMPETITIONS There are literary prizes you can enter as a small publisher. Contact Book Trust (tel 0181 870 9055) for their *Guide to Literary Prizes, Grants and Awards.*

COMPUTER-TO-PLATE Printing that does not require the making of film from origination before printing plates are made. The method of the future.

CONDENSED FACE Lettering that is narrower than a regular font.

CONTENT In the open market it is known that people often buy books on impulse and it helps if you've got a 'name'. Booksellers consider 'cover, author, quality of production' the three main criteria. Content comes later. Yet content is what will earn a place for a title in trade backlists (this is, after all, how classics are made), so content has to be outstanding.

CONTENTS These days the contents page of your book is not headed 'Table of Contents'. Neither is it called, as is sometimes mistakenly the case, 'Index'. Always make a last-proof check of page numbers in the Contents or List of Illustrations, to allow for changes resulting from that extra paragraph or picture you have added in the text.

CONVERSION Making one system compatible with another—disks can be sent to a conversion bureau for this process. Occasionally there is some corruption with words or lines lost. Be professional if this happens. The printer isn't being discriminating, s/he probably hasn't noticed and will put it right for no charge if you write the missing word or sentence in the proof.

If there is a significant amount of corruption you will have to supply another disk at your cost.

COPY Matter to be printed.

COPYRIGHT On your imprint page '© 1991 Anony Mous' is enough protection (you can also register your title at The Stationers' Company, Stationers' Hall Court, London EC4M 7DD for a small fee). Include illustrators' and collaborators' copyrights too. Acknowledgement of other copyright material used can be placed here, or it could go on one of the verso pages in the prelims.

Many self-publishers are cavalier about copyright. Think again if you want to use the logos of the Highway Code, a lovely flower design from some gift wrapping paper, or that full-colour copy of an old master in a book you have borrowed from the library. Even if an original is centuries old, a postcard reproduction you have in your possession will undoubtedly be copyrighted too.

Permissions must be obtained, fees paid, acknowledgements made as required by the original publisher. Write to permissions departments and use pictures from picture libraries if possible. Every effort must be made to trace all sources of previously published material, be it text or pictures.

The fallback position is a sentence on the imprint page saying:

> Every effort has been made to trace copyright holders and obtain permission. Any omission brought to our attention will be remedied in future editions.

The copyright of illustrations you commission yourself only belongs to you if you have paid an agreed additional fee. Otherwise illustrators must have their copyright details on the imprint page along with yours. If an illustrator appears on the title page with you as the author, he or she will share Public Lending Right payments.

Do not leave anything to chance—like the self-publisher who omitted the copyright details for her illustrator 'because it has appeared in my previous four books'.

COPYRIGHT LIBRARIES The British Library has been a library of legal deposit since 1662. Some writers publish with the sole aim of furnishing these eminent libraries with copies of their books. Some vanity publishers offer to deposit copies with the copyright libraries as an incentive for writers to use their services, despite this being an unchangeable requirement of the Copyright Protection Act. AT Smail is the agent for the copyright libraries at the universities of Oxford and Cambridge, the National Library of Scotland, the Library of Trinity College, Dublin, and the National Library of Wales. (See Legal Deposit.)

CORRECTIONS These days mistakes aren't corrected by an experienced hand as in the days of manual typesetting. Much of the processing is done electronically and mistakes like 'King Louise of France' or 'the blind Beethoven' remain until they jump out at you on the printed page.

Don't send the printer separate lists of corrections, even if you remember to include the correct paragraph and line number. Like the self-publisher who sent a bulging package of corrections written on continuous computer-label release paper, you will be charged for the extra time it takes to locate them in the text. She had decided to rewrite her book, down to unnecessary changes of single quotes to double quotes, at a very late stage.

Don't say, 'I have some very minor changes.' How can you judge whether they will be minor or whether they will create other unforeseen problems for the printer? One additional comma in a paragraph can add a full line. The 'smallest' changes take valuable computer time and they don't come free!

Printers need monosyllabic directives—do this, don't do that. Resist the temptation to apologise or explain why you are making your corrections with detailed marginal notes. Nobody is concerned with explanations, and they run the risk of being keyed into the text as requested corrections.

The best way is to have your book finished before you hand it over to a printer. Any further corrections should be made at proof stage. Whether you try to mark corrections on a proof or slip these through on telephone calls, all are chargeable as 'author's corrections'.

CORRESPONDENCE Keep correspondence with printers to an absolute minimum. Don't include proof correction instructions in letters—these should be written clearly on the proof itself. Do not use your normal handwriting but print words legibly, using capital letters only where you require them to appear. Be very concise. Use the British Standard Marks or the older printers' marks, both identified very clearly in *The Writers' Handbook*.

Always confirm your print quantity or a request for a reprint in writing.

COST How much *should* you spend? You should think in terms of £2500 for a full-length professionally designed product, depending upon extent, illustrations, type of cover and binding. After seeing production estimates, set a budget and keep to it. If necessary cut the number of pages, reduce the quantity of pictures, etc. to achieve this.

What should you make your selling price? The realistic answer is 'What is market will stand'.

Let's say you set the selling price for your book at £10. Allocate £3.50 for an average 35 per cent trade discount. If a distributor takes you on this will need to be increased to 50 per cent. Distributors undertake invoicing as well as 'repping' but you must still do the promotion. So promotion costs must be allowed—to cover press releases, review copies, printing and mailing of fliers, and maybe some small ads. This will leave at most a few pence for profit on a short print run, but don't be tempted by the more seductive cost analysis of longer runs. (See Budget.)

COURSE READERS These academic publications are ideal for short-run digital printing. They can be economic if planned in a book format, not A4.

COVERS/JACKETS An eye-catching cover or jacket plays a crucial role in the success of a book. Put on your publishing hat to oversee the design subjectively, without being too slavish to your words inside. It is a good idea to *invest* in a design by a professional artist. It might set you back as much as £200 upwards but it might also sell your book for you.

Collect suitable pictures for use or reference and draft out your back cover blurb and autobiographical notes. Finished blurb and biog should be well-crafted sales copy, and the whole design has to be customer-catching.

It is most important to devise a finished cover or jackets that will tempt complete strangers to take a second look.

It is surprising how many writers design covers using images that are lengthwise (landscape) not upright (portrait) in shape. Reduce oversize pictures and designs on a photocopier to check what impact they will make when they are a usable size.

Wrap a test dummy in A4 or A3 paper to check your cover/jacket specification. If your book is large format and especially if its extent is over 256pp (think of the width the spine has to be for 300pp), the cover will have to be printed on a faster machine at greater cost. Jackets are invariably printed on larger machines. Spine width might dictate reducing the number of pages to fit a smaller, cheaper cover size. Or plan a narrower spine to allow for adequate flaps. Your budget is the key here.

COVER PRICE Cover price is an important part of market research. Traditionally it is based on the unit cost of the print run plus promotion and administration costs. For self-publishers it is senseless embarking upon a print run of 10,000 paperbacks to make the cost of each copy low enough for its cover price to compete with Pan Macmillan's mainstream titles. Base your cover price on *what the market will stand* and be prepared to make no profit on a first short print run.

CRC see Camera-ready copy.

CROMALIN Colour proofing method that is useful for final checking before going to print.

CROP Pictures resized to delete unwanted portions. Skilful cropping can greatly increase the stylishness of a page.

CROSS-HEADS Subheads, usually centred on the page or a column of text.

CUT-AND-PASTE A useful way to plan a dummy, but dangerous to use at proof stage. Printers find it hard to follow when pictures or pieces of text are physically moved around the pages.

CUTOUT Removing the background so part of a picture is highlighted.

CUTTING Cut as much verbiage as you can and be ruthless with passages you are particularly fond of (Paul Gallico said these are the ones to banish). Before a cutting session it is a good idea not to look at your text, for several weeks if possible.

It is easy to delete on a wordprocessor. When cutting typescript use a thick felt-tip for obliteration. Once words and sentences have gone you won't be tempted by second thoughts.

Second thoughts can be crippling. A first-time writer of an 800-page novel had several bites of interest from publishers and literary agents. They all insisted the work needed stringent editorial cutting. Instead of listening to experienced reason, the writer is sure 'they're going to destroy my book'. He is on income support and can't afford photocopying, so he is searching for a way to print double-sided pages off his wordprocessor to get 'one or two perfect books' which a bookbinder has promised to bind for him at £5 each. With these he hopes to attract a backer.

Realistically his choice is simple: cut his text or cut his losses.

D

DASH see Em/En dash.

DATABASE Direct mail can often work best with a customer list you create yourself. You can store information about each name and address, such as how you were contacted. This will help you devise a demographic profile, but make sure you know the data protection guidelines by contacting the Data Protection Register (tel 01625 535777). Never be tempted to copy someone else's list into your database without permission. All rented lists have 'seed' addresses planted in them and unauthorised use is a criminal offence.

DEADLINE see Timing.

DEDICATION Try to plan your dedication page as a recto so it makes a pleasing break before the body of the book, which should also start on a recto. If spare pages are short, can you cut some of your body copy? Well-designed prelims are important (see Space).

Don't word your dedication in too emotional a manner. It will look wrong on the printed page and very personal thanks can always be sent in a letter.

DEEP LEVEL COMMANDS Embedded (formatting and printing) wordprocessor instructions. These may be instructions dedicated to your own system and they might have to be deleted before typesetting.

DELIVERY see Taking Delivery.

DEMAND PRINTING Just-in-time is a buzz word in publishing, made possible by advances brought by digital technology. So far only digital printers in the financial sector can meet tight deadlines, producing books within days. Book printers consider just-in-time to be two to six weeks.

DEPOSIT Service companies you engage will often ask for a deposit in advance. If paying in advance, it is advisable to see examples of other customers' work.

DESKTOP PUBLISHING (DTP) Computer software programs that bring type styles, graphic facilities and page design to a mass market of end users. It has caused a revolution in print management.

Acquiring a full desktop publishing system which produces camera-ready copy is very tempting because of the saving of time and cost, and the control it gives you over design. But are you sure you know enough about the conventions of good typography to design your pages to a professional standard?

Anyone in book production can spot desktop inadequacies instantly and I suspect that many sales are lost in the trade because of the telltale signs of DTP. I have seen books with four and more different typefaces on a page, five on a cover in the title alone, text peppered with italics and bold words and phrases. There are unedited typewriting habits, rivers of space throughout the text, blank lines between paragraphs, no paragraph indents and unhappy font combinations on jackets. Space-hyphen-space for dashes, three full points for ellipses, inch marks for double quotes and apostrophes for single open quotes are as much a giveaway of an amateur hand as are A5 or A4 formats.

It does not matter how powerful your desktop publishing system, the criterion is:

Have you bothered to study at least a smattering of the conventions of the art of typography?

Have you left adequate margins?

Most self-publishers do not, and they happily use their system's default A5 format which is not a book size, has ugly proportions, and can sometimes incur more cost for the cover because of the extra page width.

DESIGN Many people are design blind, just as some are tone deaf. It's a case of educating oneself. Study professional design of all descriptions—not only book jackets but magazines, brochures, annual reports, advertisements—until you can spot the difference.

Authors are not usually cover designers, and they should try not to be enslaved by their written words at visualising stage. The image you have set your heart on might not be the best one to sell the book.

Good typography can lift a mediocre cover design, but bad

typography can ruin a good one. Employ a designer and you will add value to your product beyond the fee paid.

DESKTOP PUBLISHING BUREAU Going to a DTP bureau without a planned and prepared specification could cost more than using a conventional typesetter. Shop around.

DIALECT Think carefully if you want to use dialect in fiction. A crime novel, good enough to be chosen among the Hodders and the Fabers for Scottish Book Fortnight, had limited sales elsewhere because one of the characters spoke entirely in pidgin Gaelic.

Badly done dialect is a heavy-handed way of achieving characterisation and is hard on the reader. A novel submitted on disk not only had pages and pages of dropped consonants but—a common wordprocessing fault (see Smart Key)—apostrophes standing for missing letters reproduced as single open quote marks—a nightmare for the typesetter to correct.

DIALOGUE People speak in shorthand. Listen to them and make notes. Read modern fiction to see how dialogue is handled. These days dialogue in novels and biographies is treated as a device to move the story along. A ghost writer working on an autobiography put a taped interview in the kind of words he used for his mainstream novels. His subject was delighted and the lively words increased the recall of more valuable memories.

Set out dialogue in the accepted style. Look at published novels to see where the commas fall. There is a lot wrong with the following, but it is so often seen that one wonders if it is part of the UK's English Language curriculum:

'Lets go', she said. 'There are towel's and thing's ready.' She added.

Note that very few exclamation marks are used in modern dialogue. Eliminate all 's/he said's unless absolutely necessary. When two people are talking whole pages can be uninterrupted dialogue, with very little labelling of the speakers. Phrases like 'she removed her gaze to the window', 'he quipped', 'he grinned' (as a method of speech) are outdated.

Read Graham Greene and other distinguished modern novelists to see how dialogue should move the story along. In real life people seldom speak in long passages of monologue, so keep verbiage short and to the point. Think of actors on a stage, and how they react back and forth to each other constantly.

DICTIONARY Double check with a dictionary. It is surprising how many ordinary words can be misspelt through force of habit. It is most useful and not an admission of defeat to use a spellchecker, even if you are a university graduate.

DIGITAL PRINTING This is the printing method of the future, expected to replace offset litho in the next decade. It is increasingly used for cost-effective short-run mono and colour printing. Names to look out for: DocuTech, Indigo E-Print 1000, Danka ImageSource 70, Océ Pagestream, Ricoh, Minnolta, IBM InfoPrint 4000.

With digital printing each copy is an original so 600dpi resolution can look much higher. Picture quality is good enough for general book work. Books can be archived and stored for future reprints, you can select and print parts of them only, or you can retrieve individual pages or chapters to add to other digital books. You can print from the Internet.

DIRECT SELLING Marketing direct to your customers is the simplest and most profitable method of all. There is minimal bookkeeping and no trade discount. Mail as widely as possible but expect modest results—one to two per cent sales is good. Response can be increased if you offer a price advantage, or an incentive such as a small item for enquiring only. Endorsements or testimonials in your literature can be helpful, as can a reply paid card or Freepost address.

Always follow up each communication. People often intend to respond but don't get round to it. Or you might receive useful feedback, saying why they aren't interested.

Your literature should stipulate 'receipt of goods within 28 days', with a declaration that you will fully refund anyone not satisfied with the purchase. Dissatisfied customers can contact the national media consumers' Mail Order Protection Scheme (MOPS).

Lists can be purchased from brokers and small ads taken in specialist journals. Business Database from Yellow Pages (tel 01753 583311) is a useful source of categories for non-fiction. Information on mailing list brokers can be obtained from the Direct Marketing Association (tel 0171 321 2525). Lists sell for around £40–£300 plus per 1000 addresses. Don't overlook your own customer base built up over time. If you are mailing to over 4000 UK addresses, contact your local Royal Mail Business Centre for bulk mailing discounts. 'The Royal Mail Guide to Successful Door to Door' can be obtained by ringing Freefone 0800 581939.

DIRECT-TO-PRINT Nowadays it is possible to print direct from computer in methods as widely different as digital short-run and sheet (and web) offset long-run printing. But you must be able to produce PostScript print files.

DISCOUNT see Trade Discount.

DISK (DISC) There are many forms of disk in small and large capacity for storing data. Purchase a proven brand, otherwise files might be corrupted or lost within a period of time.

DISPATCH An advantage small publishers have over large publishers is the speed at which copies can be dispatched to purchasers. Don't mail in used envelopes. Purchase protective envelopes in bulk to save cost or, better still, use small collapsible boxes.

DISTRIBUTION This is the most difficult part of self-publishing. It is unlikely that you will be able to afford the services of a rep or distributor and you will have to take on marketing, invoicing and delivery yourself. However there is no harm in sending distributors an early copy to see if they will take their title into their list. But if they do, don't become so excited that you deliver 5000 copies of your book and are stuck with warehousing fees for years ahead.

Distributors need advance information three months before publication date. Some firms offer PR and marketing. However titles must be worth their while—it is unlikely that a distributor will show interest in low-profile local books or unedited first novels.

Distributors take a percentage for invoicing and dispatching above the booksellers' discount and charge for warehousing. You won't see much change on early sales for yourself, and payment is in arrears—after the bookseller pays the distributor, which can be ninety days or longer. Distributors for small publishers sometimes advertise in *The Bookseller* magazine (obtainable from J Whitaker & Son on subscription). Or you can approach them individually at the London International Book Fair.

DOUBLE QUOTES Normally used for quotes within quotes:
'It surprised me when the holy man used "like some buried Caesar" in such perfect English.'

DOUBLE SPREAD Matter (often a picture or pictures) printed across two facing pages. Needs planning care, especially with short-run printing.

DRAFT You will have made many of these before passing your book 'ready to print'. Redrafting copy may be an onerous task but it must be done to save heavy author's correction charges later on. Printers' proofs are not drafts and should not be used to get your book into shape.

DROP Space above the first line of a page or column of text. Often used with good effect at chapter heads.

DROP CAPS More often used in magazine than book publishing, in which it can give an old-fashioned look.

DROP-IN Printer's term meaning insert.

DTP see Desktop Publishing.

DUES Orders that have been subscribed in advance of publication. When copies are in the retailers' hands you might have to wait for payment for up to three months. If you are using a distributor there might be a further wait of a few weeks. So don't count money due to you as yours until it is banked. Even then there may be returns and the retailers (and distributor) will want their money back.

DUMMY A mock-up of a book which is very useful at planning stage. Make a dummy to help you decide how to get the best package out of your budget. Do you need to cut words and/or illustrations? Would your market prefer a larger thinner book? Or should you consider fewer pages on bulkier paper? A dummy will help you to plan your cover or jacket to an economic size for printing.

DUMPBINS Display containers for books, often badged with publishers' imprints. At least one actively motivated Writers' Circle is selling members' publications in dumpbins in their locality.

DUPE Copy from a transparency. Can be made in colour or in black-and-white (b/w).

E

ECONOMY OF WORDS 'If it is possible to cut a word, always cut it out.' (George Orwell *Politics and the English*

Language 1946) 'Say it as simply as possible.' (*The Economist* style sheet 1986).

EDITING Tightening your text will save pages *and* printing cost—many self-publishers leave the don't-touch-a-comma-of-my-writing school when they see how much of the cost of production is a per-page cost. At the same time, good editing makes your book a more professional product. Repetition and rambling should be cut in non-fiction. In fiction don't allow characters to gaze at each other before speaking, quip hilariously, or speak for paragraphs in lecturing or hectoring tones. Avoid too much minutiae and/or an obtrusive narrator voice.

Books produced before DTP changed writers' lives invariably had the attention of a typesetter who kept to the rule book and saved many of the literals we see in text today. Alas, theirs is a dying art. If you can find a secondhand copy of *Rules for Compositors and Readers at the Oxford University Press* you will find it an invaluable aid (a limited edition has been reprinted recently).

To have your book professionally edited will undoubtedly cost money (from £11 an hour). But it could mean the fulcrum upon which notice of your book—as a professional one in an oversubscribed world—is taken seriously by reviewers and the trade.

Good editing saves money in the end and always produces a better book.

EDITION The form which a particular title takes, identified by the two or three last digits in its international standard book number (ISBN) —'8-3' for this edition of *Bring It To Book*. A hardback edition of an original paperback requires a new ISBN and vice versa. If you spot glaring mistakes in your first edition that warrant the cost of a corrected edition, this will also need a new number. If you want the printer to delete a few commas and correct Aunt Flo to Auntie Flo for a reprint, or if you redesign the cover to include some good reviews on the back, you keep the same number.

EDITOR There are different types of editor. In professional terms: commissioning editors give valuable help and advice; line editors will do a full edit which might include restructuring and continuity; copy editors concentrate on style, consistency and punctuation. Authors commissioned by a publishing house receive these services at no charge. When you are originating your book yourself you must put on all these editing hats if you want your product to compete with theirs in the wider world. Or you could commission a freelance editor for a quality product.

ELLIPSIS The three full points that signify a word or part of a word is omitted. To be professional use the 'smart key' in your page composition system. In this typeface a correct ellipsis is '…', not '...'.

EM & EN Printers' measures based on the size of an 'M' or 'N' in a font—there is an em space between the glossary headings and their explanations in this book, not two key strokes. This keeps the distance constant. Mark it for typesetting as 'M' or 'N' within circles (see page 19).

EM DASHES The correct form of dash for punctuation. The ASCII code for an em dash is <197> giving —; for an en dash it is <196> giving –. Like ems, different fonts have differently sized dashes, e.g. — (13pt Bookman) and — (8pt Avant Garde). An en dash is more stylish for 1790–1820 than a hyphenated 1790-1820. You might find these as 'Smart Key' symbols in your page composition system.

EMBOSS To raise or impress a design (effective on a book cover).

EMULSION The coating on a photograph or printer's film. It is easily scratched off, especially on the latter. If you are providing film for a printer to use, ask how they require it—if it should be 'emulsion side down', for instance.

END MATTER Information that comes after the main body of the text, often in the following order:
  appendices
  endnotes and references
  bibliography
  glossary
  index

ENDNOTES see End Matter. Sometimes advertisements of other books by the same author or publisher can be included as a last item.

END PAPER Sheets of paper at the front and back of a book. Sometimes they are patterned or coloured (darker colours are more expensive than lighter ones). Paperbacks with coloured (or patterned) ends can look stylish, especially for poetry.

ENDS see End Paper.

ENLARGE see Blow Up and Scale.

ENVELOPES *Always* send artwork or pictures through the post in card-backed envelopes or use a piece of card in an ordinary envelope. Write 'Please do not bend' on the outside. Don't post books in unprotected envelopes, even ones that fit like a glove. Use jiffy bags or protect with bubblewrap. Better still, use small boxes, especially for multiple copies. Don't tape the package up in such a way that it takes an unnecessary amount of time to break into it.

EPILOGUE Most books don't need an epilogue but if you are using one, spend time in wording it to give it a *raison d'être*. To begin, 'In closing, let me say...', is too rambling and chatty.

EPOS (Electronic Point of Sale) Nowadays a keystroke of a lightpen can retrieve information about a book from a bar code. Most booksellers are on an EPOS system so it is wise to include a bar code on your cover, or sometimes the back flap of a jacket.

ERRORS Many books I see in the course of business are not ready for publication, let alone presenting to a printer. It seems errors and omissions only jump out at self-publishers when the text appears in the new dimension of the printed page. Then writers start the polishing which should have been done in the form of drafts in their wordprocessors, sometimes paying the cost of nine proofs to purge stray commas.

Errors missed in the first proof are chargeable if marked for correction in a subsequent proof, when they can be as high as '£1 a line', rising to '£1 a key stroke' and above.

One author-publisher had a sleepless night paging through the classics to discover if the placing of two words he was desperate to transpose at the last minute had been used in his original position by any eminent author. They had—by Shelley. So he felt justified in saving the expense. (In common with most last-minute corrections, no one else would have noticed the need for change.)

ESTIMATES An indication of cost based on specification given. Printers should keep to estimates (within the time limit they have set for its validity) unless your specifications change, or the copy doesn't match them.

It is best to have a clear idea of all requirements for a job specification so that printers' estimates can truly reflect the product you have in mind. You must, for instance, indicate if your book has an index, bibliography and reference notes. Such pages (give a realistic number) require more expensive typesetting—as do tables and text in columns. Count these and indicate them separately.

Make a note of how many different style headings and subheads are to be used and if you require running heads or footnotes. Give an accurate number of illustrations and say whether you want them reproduced in halftone or line, whether they will be supplied as originals (e.g. photographs), embedded as computerised images in your text, or whether they will be supplied as digital scans on disk.

You must have a clear idea (and preferably a rough to submit) of what your cover or jacket design will look like before estimating. Printers need to know whether the artwork is to be supplied on disk, as 'camera-ready' or is it to be made up by them. They need to know the quantity and type of pictures and the number of colours. One- or two-colour covers can be very successful if the artwork and typography are excellent—look at Faber & Faber covers.

The form your book will take will begin to decide itself, after a thorough understanding of all the costs involved, not least because of your budget restrictions. The largest publishers compromise where necessary and so should you.

EVEN-WORKING Traditional even-working is the exact number of pages the printer can print from plates of 16, 32 or 64 pages. Digital printing allows multiples of 4 pages. It can be difficult to decide whether to go for the more flexible new digital short-run printing, or for a longer print run by traditional means—when the more copies you have the less each one will cost (supposing you sell them all).

EXCLAMATION MARK Be very sparing in the use of this mark and never double it, except if quoting a previously published passage, or a letter.

EXHIBITIONS Look out for book fairs and organisations (such as the Independent Publishers' Guild and the British Council) which offer shared exhibition space. Authors of specialist subjects—and some novelists—can have success at craft (and other) fairs, and at least one septuagenarian sells his war memoirs successfully at boot fairs.

EXPANDED A face in a font family that is stretched out. A useful style in cover design.

EXPENSES There are several legitimate expenses you can claim against tax when publishing a book, such as stationery, fares, research journals and reference books, contributors and copyright fees. Don't forget to claim membership subscriptions to the associations or societies you belong to, including Writers' Circles. Ask your accountant what receipts you should keep.

EXPORTING There are several ways to export books. You can sell rights to a foreign publisher, sell on the Internet, sell through an exporting bookseller or distributor, or negotiate an arrangement with an overseas stock-holding agent.

Shipping must be handled professionally and you will have to become familiar with the difference between cost, insurance and freight (CIF) and free-on-board (FOB) options. Contact the trade departments of embassies and high commissions, and the British Council (tel 0171 930 8466).

EXTENT The number of pages your book makes. Larger printers might charge less for 256pp than 248pp because the former allows 'even-working'—printing all sections in multiples of 32pp. There are high-tech methods geared to multiples of 4 pages but stick to 16- or 32-page planning if you foresee longer-run reprints.

The book's extent and its trimmed size (called format) dictate the printer's price range. Keep within manageable limits. Design your book 'demy octavo'—216 x 135mm—or under and to an 'even-working' extent, and you can make a considerable saving in cost.

For example a self-publisher had a text-only book of over 500 pages. He was very pleased that he had written so much and hoped to put a high cover price on the book. But a paperback by an unknown author could not carry a reasonable cover price that would recoup production costs on a short print run. Paper alone was a significant cost.

The extra width of the spine meant that the cover had to be printed on a larger machine at greater cost. He would have been better off with a 256-page book.

F

FEATHERING see Vertical Justification.

FICTION Self-published fiction *is* possible to sell, particularly to local booksellers and to libraries, and it can be well reviewed, occasionally in the nationals. *It must be well edited*—remember how many established novelists give thanks to their editors at prize-giving ceremonies (also how books by household name publishers are often slated for sloppy editing or proofreading in reviews).

FILE Computer data that can be 'opened' and 'read'. It can be the text for a whole book, a letter, page composition style, PostScript print information, or a full-colour cover on disk.

FILM Negatives or positives used in offset printing. There has to be a separate film for each colour of ink to be printed.

FINISHED ART Artwork that is ready for printing, whether it is a complete cover or just the completed illustration for the front.

FLAP The 'turn in' pieces of a book jacket. These should be generous in width to allow them to stay flat when the book is opened. Most jackets are printed on SRA2 machines to allow the extra width required for flaps.

FLIER/MAILSHOT A flier is a useful piece of promotional literature. If you are placing small ads, be they only a few lines of copy, you will need something professional to send to respondents. You should mail out information about your book well in advance of publication date. The design for the front cover should be decided at an early stage (reduced in size if necessary), so it can form side 1 of a promotional flier.

Side 2 of the flier will need some good 'selling' copy and can include an order form. It must also feature the essentials of price, ISBN, publication date, number of pages, size, whether hardback or paperback, number and type of illustrations. Firming up on these details will allow you to complete Whitaker's book information form, another important aspect of advance information.

On the first edition of your flier you can say 'publication: summer 1998', instead of 'May 1998'. The unpredictable often happens in book publishing and you can always firm up the date later. You can use the Shelwing service for mailing fliers to libraries, library suppliers, and booksellers (call Elaine Marshall on 01303 850501 for *their* flier).

If you can afford it, have fliers with side 1 in full colour to promote a book with a full-colour cover or jacket. If you can't, most covers will translate into an acceptable black-and-white halftone reproduction (at much less cost), but say somewhere that the actual cover or jacket is in full colour.

I know self-publishers who leave a trail of fliers wherever they go. They should of course have temptation written all over them—your front cover reproduction must be eye-stopping, even as a thumbnail in black and white.

FLUSH/PERFECT Glue-bound paperbacks. Long-run binding is stronger than short-run binding simply because the machines have more advanced features.

FOIL There is a vogue for foil-embossing on books. This is commonly gold or silver but can be any colour, or even patterned effects. If you go direct to a foil-embossing company

A flier with side 1 in colour and side 2 in black-and-white (kind permission of Forest Lodge Scotland DD8 4QN)

it can be surprisingly inexpensive, but allow for spoils in your print order.

FOLIOS Page numbers. The term originates from folded-section printing. New digital short-run presses print pages already collated with no folding and gathering required, but you might still find the old name being used.

FONT FAMILY A typeface in its versions of roman, italic, bold, condensed, expanded, etc.

FOOT The bottom of a page, cover, etc.

FOOTNOTES Explanations at the end of a page. Some DTP and wordprocessing packages run footnotes automatically, but you can also identify the text in question with superscript numbers and include their explanations at the end of chapters. I have seen each page's footnotes ranged left down the outer margins in a coffee-table book with lots of stylish white space. Expensive but effective.

Footnotes are sparingly used these days but there is a self-publisher whose footnotes are two-thirds of a page long and they had to be placed in special hidden frames. Luckily it was not the spiritual book whose footnotes vanished inexplicably in the second proof, except for the name of the medium's guide. This printed in letters nearly an inch high at right angles to the normal text—and there was no program in that particular book for rotated setting!

FOREIGN WORDS & PHRASES In the heat of the moment writers use foreign language words, dash off foreign phrases or drop famous names in cavalier fashion without bothering to double-check how they are spelt. Mistakes like 'C'et Larouse' used to be corrected as a matter of course by old-fashioned typesetters.

Don't italicise foreign words and phrases in common use, like vis-à-vis, rendezvous, vice versa, quid pro quo. Never use quotation marks *and* italics.

FOREWORD A piece about the author. It is useful to have this written by someone else, the more well known the better. Give a deadline with plenty of leeway—I know several author–publishers waiting for distinguished names to flag on front covers dangerously close to publication date. Don't let your book be published with Foreword called Forward.

FORMAT The trimmed size a book (also the term for the arrangement and parameters of computer data, not applicable for inclusion in this book). It is always better to tailor your system to produce a professional book format than use its default A5 and A4 sizes. Book sizes were established long before 'A' sizes came into being. In general terms books under 216 x 135mm (which is demy octavo format) can be printed for significantly less than books in larger sizes.

different book formats ...

If paperback, their covers can be printed at less cost on smaller machines.

Many self-publishers are injudicious about format, ignoring the fact that booksellers and libraries have shelves of a certain height. Neither market resistance nor the cost factor deterred one would-be self-publisher who wanted to produce an A3-sized children's book because some of the (undisclosed) subject matter had to be life-size. Few booksellers or libraries will stock an A3-sized children's book 'because the subject matter needs to be life-size'. They think in terms of shelf space and can't pander to the eccentricity of authors.

Booksellers and librarians do not like A4-sized books, other than for technical manuals. For larger books they prefer the professional royal octavo format (234 x 154mm).

Standard cost-effective book sizes are:
Demy octavo (216 x 135mm); C format (210 x 135mm); B format like this book (198 x 128mm); A format ('Penguin size', 180 x 110mm).
A5 makes an ugly book size but falls into this group.

The width of paper used (whether sheet- or reel-fed) is significant. A few millimetres too large in format and your job will have to go on a larger machine at greater cost to you. Better to plan the most economic overall package and then tailor your words to fit.

FOUR-COLOUR PROCESS Four colours used to reproduce colour originals that have been screened. The process colours are black, magenta, cyan and yellow. Screening allows many combinations of overlapping colour in different weights to give a full-colour result.

FRACTIONS Study the manual for your wordprocessor to find out how to present fractions correctly if you are originating camera-ready copy. You could find them on Smart Keys on your keyboard. Typesetters might prefer you to indicate where they occur on hard copy, or later in a proof, because their coding system might be different to yours.

FRAMES An invisible box in a page composition system that holds text or pictures.

FREELANCE A useful source of help for small publishers. Designers, artists, editors, picture researchers and production people can all be hired by the hour, or by a price for the job.

FULL COLOUR Printing process that reproduces a colour original in four or more colours.

FULL POINT Printers' term for full stop. Full points are not used after Mrs, Dr, Prof, and so on. They are also omitted from acronyms: ALCS, BPIF, PLR, and often from initials: WH Smith.

FULL OUT Copy that is set flush to the left with no indent, like these paragraphs.

G

GALLEY PROOF The text of a book in a continuous column, without page breaks. This was the way proofs were set before the age of computer page make-up systems and desktop publishing, which go 'straight to page'.

GATHER Assembly of collated sheets, or folded sections, of a book before binding.

GHOST An unnamed writer who composes someone else's idea or story into words.

GHOSTING Missing or light areas of colour in a print job (see Solid).

GLOSSARY Definitions in alphabetical order. Often used

to explain foreign words/phrases or technical terms. You shouldn't find it necessary to explain commonly used words or items especially in works of fiction.

GLUE-BINDING Glue-binding has improved for paperbacks in the last decade. Slimmer copies are cheaper to bind because they require less glue and fewer boxes for packing. The longer the print run, the stronger the binding and the lower the unit cost.

Always have extra covers and papercases printed to allow for spoils at make-ready (even jackets for jacketing).

GRAIN The direction in which the fibres of paper or board run. Long grain runs parallel to the long edge of the paper. In a ream of paper with its size indicated, the long grain figure comes first. For best results pages and covers should be printed with the grain running lengthwise, otherwise covers won't lie flat and pages will curl or 'buckle'. Many digital printers print two-to-view books on the short grain. Their books could be improved if they bound the pages on the outside edge, not centrally. There are ways to achieve this very easily.

GRAMMAGE Weight of stock (paper or board).

GRAMMAR Good grammar means easier communication. Take control of your sentences. Shorten them and construct them well to express yourself with clarity. Go back to basics with a refresher course—it is dangerous to think that because you can write a letter, you can write a book.

GRAPHIC An image or design created in, or imported into, a computer program.

GREEKING Dummy type to give the effect of typesetting. Useful for layouts.

GRID Sheets marked with faint lines (usually blue) used

for paste-up of artwork or text before the advent of computerised page make-up systems and desktop publishing.

GRIP The edge that cannot be printed due to mechanical requirements in some processes, similar to the 'blind' margin when photocopying. It is about 10mm on one specified edge of the paper. Allow for it if your printer asks you to.

GSM Thickness of card expressed in grammes per square metre, e.g. 240gsm or 240g/m^2.

GUTTER The two inside margins of a book. If you are designing your pages yourself, make sure you leave enough gutter to allow for binding, especially for short-run paperbacks.

H

HALFTONE 'Full tone value' black-and-white reproduction of photographs/watercolours, etc.

HALF-TITLE The first page of a book. (See Prelims.)

HANGING INDENT Style to use for tabular matter, displayed like Further Reading and the index in this book.

HARDBACK These days your dream hardback could be easier to sell as a (more affordable) paperback. Even libraries prefer paperbacks in many instances because they cost less for overstrained purchasing budgets. But hardbacks can make more profit for small publishers. This is because the additional cost for boards and casing-in is not as high as the increase you can add to the cover price. Hardbacks come in many different styles. Top-of-the-range is a leather-bound edition with headbanding and ribbon. Roundbacks are more attractive (and more expensive than straightbacks). Thread-sewn hardbacks are stronger than glued hardbacks (and more expensive). There is more than one method of sewing. Papercased hardbacks are a cost-effective option because they don't require expensive jacket printing. However, because of the extra time required to manufacture hardbacks and because of possible restricted sales, it is wise to learn the ins and outs of publishing with a paperback edition first.

HEAD The top of a page, cover, etc.

HEADBANDING Ribbon trim at the head of a cased book. Looks classy but is expensive.

HEADINGS see Subheads.

HOOK-IN Indenting, especially in lines of poetry. Poets usually know exactly how they want their work laid out and are very particular in their use of punctuation. Hook-ins should be achieved by em and en spaces, not spacebar spaces.

HOUSE STYLE Conventions that ensure consistency in phrasing and style. Each publishing house has its own variations but many of the requirements are standard.

HOWEVER Restrict the use of this adverb. You'll be surprised how seldom it is needed when you weed it out. Try 'but' or 'yet' instead (see Short Words).

HYPHENS ('SOFT') End-of-line hyphens are computer-generated and improve the look of typeset lines. Too often writers agonise about end-of-line hyphens. They react as if split words are mutilation and a hyphenated last word on a page, decapitation. After two years' experience of self-publishers, our rule became 'no soft hyphens for anyone over the age of sixty, even if their text is littered with unnecessary hard hyphens'.

A younger writer went to the expense of litigation over the use of end-of-line hyphens. If you remain pathological about end-of-line hyphens, ask for the text to be set with 'hyphenation off'. The typesetting won't look as nice, but it will save you making yourself appear foolish when you count them as 'printers' errors' or stand up in the Small Claims Court to say they make your words unreadable.

Margaret Atwood and Evelyn Waugh novels (and any other 'name' author you care to mention) have end-of-line and end-of-*page* hyphens. Their words are prepared and honed to perfection, whatever the splits. Are yours?

HYPHENS ('HARD') Manually keyed hyphens in a) hyphenated words and b) unfinished words at the end of lines in your wordprocessor. If your text is going to be typeset, the typesetter's line endings are likely to be different from yours. All split words will have to be joined up and the hard hyphens removed—a legitimate author's correction charge by the typesetter. Using too many hyphenated words is old-fashioned.

'To-day' and 'week-end' for instance should be 'closed up' as single words. There should be no hyphen after a colon (':' not ':-').

I

ILLUSTRATIONS Resist the temptation to include every relevant picture you own if your book is illustrated. Pictures should be cut just as superfluous text should be cut. I quoted once for 'say thirty six illustrations' in a non-fiction book. We were sent over 100 drawings, each stapled into a separate plastic grocery bag. Apart from the physical effort of retrieving them from the bags, it seemed to us that the drawings of poorer quality would detract rather than contribute any value to the finished product.

'No, I want them all in—they are *my* collected work,' said the author.

Print is not a black art which just 'happens'. There are logistical problems in locating, sizing and positioning thirty six or 100 pictures—let alone the 320 cartoons which another author wanted to include in his self-help book. A professional cartoonist had completed fifty to the author's brief before giving up. Another 270 drawings would push the extent to over 400 pages. Browsers in bookshops would be intimidated, and the chosen cover price was too low for the production to break even.

Decide at an early stage if illustrations warrant excellent reproduction on art paper. Or can they be run on the same paper as the text, although this will mean they are reproduced in slightly lower quality? It'll make a significant difference to the cost, especially for a short print run. The better your originals the better the result will be for any print job.

At planning stage, illustrations can be reduced to size on a photocopier and pasted in roughly where they are required. Transworld makes children's picture book dummies like this as rights' copies to offer at Frankfurt Book Fair.

You must seek permission from the artist or publisher of any previously published illustrations you intend to use. There is copyright in all artistic works and you must always gain permission before you use them.

IMPOSITION The way in which pages are positioned for printing in different formats—generally 32-, 16-, or 8-page impositions, but digital short-run printing can be four pages printed in one pass.

IMPRINT This is the name you choose as a publisher. If you are publishing only one title for limited circulation, it is simpler when paying in at the bank, if this is in your own name. If you don't want to give yourself away as a self-publisher, ask your bank the implications of trading under an imprint name.

You can choose any name you like for your imprint. It should sound professional—you might grow to publish more books. It also looks professional if you have a logo designed. But if you decide upon Hogarth Press (as Virginia and Leonard

Pages of a book imposed for printing four pages on each side of a single sheet of paper. Photocopy and fold across three times to achieve the effect of an eight-page section

Woolf did to self-publish their short stories), you will probably find the ISBN Agency will advise against it.

It is a legal requirement to state the name and addresses of the publisher and printer in your book. It's best not to use a box number, although this is not uncommon. If you manage to find a distributor you could include their name for extra credibility (a few orders may come from the book itself). Think of designing a publisher's mark or logo to make an impact on the spine and title page.

IMPRINT PAGE Usually page 4 (unnumbered), the verso of the title page, carrying all the publishing and copyright details for your book (see the fourth page in this book).

IN PRO Picture planning that allows originals to be reduced, or enlarged, in the same batch. It saves cost but it requires some experience to select originals of different dimensions to share a finished image width. Using a slide rule is helpful.

INDENT
   Text that is set inside the text measure, like this paragraph (see Hook-In).

Indent the first lines of paragraphs by using an em space (or even a tab setting), not key strokes.

INDEX Subjects, names, book titles, etc. listed alphabetically with relevant page numbers—normally the last pages in a book.

Some self-published non-fiction books are impressively researched, but they have no bibliographies or indexes. You might have an indexing facility in your wordprocessor, or you can purchase an automatic software package to make indexing less labour-intensive, even if it only lists items by page numbers and you have to design the columns yourself. Check professionally published books to see how indexes are laid out. Also note the style for numbering consistency, i.e. 172–7 (adopted for this book although not strictly correct for a glossary). Good indexing needs a skilled hand (contact the Society of Indexers, tel 0171 916 7809, for professional help).

INITIAL CAPS Be sparing with capitalised nouns such as 'King', 'Officer', 'Government', unless being very specific, e.g. King George V.

INITIALS Initials should be free of full points: USA not U.S.A., OBE not O.B.E., OK not O.K., BSc not B.S.c.

INSERT Instruction to the printer to add text or pictures. Text or images that have to be added to existing matter should be marked 'insert here', not cut and physically moved to another location in a proof, with no indication of what has been done. Inserts are also sheets added to printed pages or a section of colour plates (see Tip-in).

INSET A small image positioned within a larger one, often used for maps or diagrams.

INTERNET The global network of computers, most commonly linked by telephone lines, to share information. You can market your book on the Internet. It will cost approx £150–£300pa for a published title depending upon which web site you choose. Discover how many sales—or failing that, hits—are received per month, and shop around.

INTRODUCTION A piece exclusively about the subject of the book. Keep it short. This book has a long introduction because the body copy is a fragmented glossary.

INVOICE You can walk into bookshops with a few copies of your book and a duplicate invoice book bought in a local stationers. Or you can have special forms headed 'Invoice & Statement' with your imprint name and address and the following columns listed across them:

REF*	QTY	TITLE & ISBN	PRICE	DISC%	VALUE	P&P	VAT RATE
(*Ref here is the *buyer's* reference)		(a)	(b)		(c)	(d)	(e)

a) List (cover/selling) price
b) Discount percentage, e.g. 35%
c) Value (a minus b)
d) Quite legitimate to charge for dispatching single orders.
e) VAT rate = zero (You must show this if you are VAT registered).

At the bottom show Total Amount Due, below a £0.00 VAT figure. Don't forget to date and number your invoice/statement (it is good practice to send these as one document)

Once you are in Whitaker's lists you might receive computerised orders (TeleOrdering). You will need to quote the buyer's order number in your reference column (or write it in your invoice book) and possibly to send a delivery order with the books and the invoice to 'head office'. Doing just as bookshop managers (or order forms) ask will speed up payment.

Print a strict policy for prompt payment on your forms (or use labels from stationers in your invoice book), being a clear statement that action will be taken after the period has expired. In many instances you will have to send reminders. Take action after the second reminder.

ISBN Apply early for your international standard book number. Having an ISBN is not a legal requirement but allows easy access to your book.

The digits are made up of country of origin, publisher's prefix and the unique string for your title (list price is not included in a simple number) and is essential to the increasing number of booksellers and most libraries which operate electronic point of sale (EPOS). It is used for Public Lending Right, and will allow Whitaker's *Books in Print* to consider your title in their comprehensive lists.

It will let you join the ranks of active publishers—it is small publishing which is a growth market in many countries.

But you are not committed to publish with an ISBN. There is no need to register your imprint or form a company (don't be tempted to call yourself Book Press *Ltd* just because it sounds good—the use of 'Ltd' is illegal for anything but an incorporated company).

Write under your imprint name to the International Standard Book Numbering Agency Ltd at 12 Dyott Street, London WC1A 1DF. There is no charge for a publisher prefix and the first number (a log book of ten numbers costs under £50). You need to give them the firm title, subtitle if any, and the author's name. Equally important is the address you will use as publisher and your publishing name. You must also give a contact name and phone number (and address if different from the one you are using as publisher).

The International Standard Book Numbering Agency requires copies of the title page, imprint page and contents page. You can wait to send these with your completed Whitaker book information form if they are not yet completed. You will receive this blue form within about two weeks in a package with useful information and a letter giving you your first number. It is easier to apply for subsequent numbers than to try and work them out yourself as they suggest.

A refugee who didn't speak much English wasn't enthusiastic when he received *his* package from Whitaker's.

'Now I must get permission,' he stated flatly.

'What permission?'

'Of course, government permission.'

He was delighted when I pointed out that in a democracy he required no permission from anybody to publish. But now his book solving algebraic equations of high degree is out, the restraints of academic censorship seem to be less democratic to him than in Russia, where selling his permitted books was easy.

ISBN AGENCY The UK International Standard Book Numbering Agency is part of Whitaker's Bibliographic Service. When you apply for an ISBN send the following information:

Name of publisher/imprint exactly as quoted on the book

The full UK postal address of the publisher

- telephone/fax numbers and e-mail address (if available)
- The name of the person at the publishing address who will be responsible for the ISBNs
- VAT number if applicable
- An estimate of how many differing titles will be published in a twelve-month period
- A photocopy/rough draft of the title page and its verso which should include a clear 'published by' statement

ISDN Check with your printer before transfering data by electronic means

ISSN International Standard Series Number for serials (magazines and journals).

ITALICS Don't call it 'slanty writing'. And don't use too much of it. Like the new novelist whose dialogue was entirely in italics because she thought it looked nice. Any words requiring emphasis in italic passages should be set in roman. Printers will set underlined words in italics.

J

JACKET Jackets are more expensive to print than covers. Because of their horizontal width they have to be printed on larger machines—you can say goodbye to a short print run when the operator presses the button, and the cost will be greater. To spine width add 6mm. To page width add 3mm (front and back). Add 3mm to height (head and foot). Allow 5mm for fore-edge wrap (round the boards), front and back. Flaps should be generous enough not to spring up when the book is opened (say 10–12mm). Allow sufficient bleed all round and, when printed, send jackets to the bookbinder untrimmed.

JARGON Jargon can be used with good effect in fiction but don't explain obvious words within brackets. Use it sparingly in non-fiction, where you should communicate as clearly

A demy octavo Scriptmate Editions' jacket printed by offset litho in full colour. Note the extra width compared with the cover in the same format on page 37. A papercase would be printed on the same size paper as the cover and is therefore cheaper than a jacket. Good reviews were received in time to include on the back but, although the title was selected for Scottish Book Fortnight, a new author in this category (crime) should not have been published in hardback in this format. It should have been a paperback in smaller A or B format (cover photo by Michael Davies)

as possible. (Printers jealously guard their jargon and are disdainful towards customers who don't use basic terminology.)

JOB Printers' term for a specific piece of work-in-hand.

JOB BAG Container (usually a very large envelope) for all the separate pieces relating to a job.

JOBBING PRINTER A printer who does not print books. An increasing number of jobbing printers will be offering a book service using digital presses. If you decide to use a jobbing printer, ask to see samples to make sure they can produce a satisfactory book product.

JUSTIFY Spacing of letters to the exact text measure, like the paragraphs of this book. Typesetters prefer word-processed text to come to them unjustified (with hyphenation 'off'). Their own measure is unlikely to give the same end-of-line hyphens as your software, and yours will have to be corrected, extra work that is chargeable. Often work you do on your computer will have to be undone and it would have been better to have composed the text like an old-fashioned letter, 'ragged right'.

K

KERNING Adjustment of spacing between characters to achieve a good visual effect. Many wordprocessors have automatic kerning but some letter pairs require extra attention. Unkerned = AV. Kerned = AV.

KEYLINE Fine lines used by designers to indicate where pictures or text are to fall, the position of a colour picture, or a bar code on cover artwork, etc.

L

LAMINATE A gloss or matt (usually more expensive) finish

to covers. Allow extra covers to compensate for make-ready spoils. If your cover is to have gold, silver or coloured foil, make sure lamination is done after the foil blocking. A major book printer didn't and the customer was embarrassed by the title and her name slipping off copies as they were touched.

Always allow for spoils at make-ready in your print run for covers, jackets or papercases. To be safe allow 100 extras to accommodate binding set-up as well.

LANDSCAPE Pictures or text set perpendicular to the height of a page. Landscape full-page pictures should face into and away from the gutter for left- and right-hand pages respectively.

LARGE PRINT Books set in a large typeface (e.g. 13–17pt) is a market which can be tapped profitably by self-publishers. One of our customers has a corner reserved for her large print books in her local branch of WH Smith. Others have sold large print secondary rights. But large print means more pages and more pages mean extra origination and printing cost.

LAY You might hear a printer say, 'Lay to left, strip to short edge'. You might have to take account of this when positioning your image, so ask what it means.

LAYOUT Images planned on a computer screen or an arrangement of text and pictures on a page.

LEADING (pronounced 'ledding') In the days of hot metal, strips of lead or brass were used as spacers, hence the term 'leading' for the space between lines of type. (See Line Feed.)

LEAD TIME Make your lead time to publication date as far ahead of the delivery date of your books as you possibly can. Six to eight weeks is a minimum—distributors and libraries require three to four months to send out advance notice of a new title.

LEAF A piece of paper with a page on either side.

LEGAL DEPOSIT A copy of each edition of your book (e.g. hardback and paperback carrying different ISBNs) must be lodged with the British Library at Legal Deposit Office, The British Library, Boston Spa, Wetherby, West Yorkshire LS23 7BY as soon as possible. You can wait until their agent AT Smail contacts you for copies for the other five legal deposit libraries, or send them to him at 100 Euston Street, London NW1 2HQ.

LETTERING Words, for example a title on a cover (never call it writing). 'My book only needs writing on its cover—it will sell itself,' is not a good idea—unless you employ a skilled typographer.

LETTERPRESS Printing method using raised blocks of type. Overtaken by offset litho (which is now being threatened by digital technology).

LETTER SPACING Space added between letters to correct loose spacing between words, which often happens when end-of-line hyphenation is turned off. Hyphenation 'on' is the better solution. In typesetting the letter 'i' is given less space than the letter 'm' or 'e', unlike the equal space given by typewriters or dot matrix printers. Therefore you can never predict what will actually happen when you add last-minute changes to your text.

LIBEL Publishing a statement or a picture which could bring its subject into disrepute. Until the law is changed, printers are as responsible as publishers in litigation. There is a man doing the rounds of printers with a book against which he *wants* someone to bring an action to publicise his case. He is known to be top-bracket rich but so far no printer has taken on the job.

LIBRARIES Each library authority is a law unto itself—

what one deplores another will welcome. Nowadays the purchasing policy of many public libraries' acquisition departments can be 'lots or none'. But all are committed to encouraging writers, so keep trying. Your own library headquarters will be approachable because you are a local author.

Stock editors of the 200+ public library headquarters welcome information about books but they like to receive advance information and/or covers/jackets/fliers, three to four months before publication date. If your title is academic non-fiction, don't forget to put research and university libraries on your list.

LIBRARY SUPPLIERS It is easier to sell through library suppliers than individual libraries (except those in your region). Send them a copy of your book with your advance information at least six weeks before publication date.

It is encouraging when a library supplier orders and pays for, say, forty copies, but some of these books (sent 'on approval' to district library headquarters, or displayed in library suppliers' book centres) could be returned to you.

LIGHT FACE Weight of typeface not as heavy as 'regular' or 'bold'.

LIMP The professional term for paperback binding. Can be sewn with a 'drawn on' cover. (See Glue Binding.)

LINE Drawings, diagrams, etc. with no tonal values.

LINE FEED Interline spacing, taken from the base of one line to the base of the next, in points. This book is set in an 11pt font with 13pt line feed. Spacing such as 'nine on eleven point' and 'eleven on thirteen' (as in this book)—expressed 9/11pt, 11/13pt—is now computer-generated. (See Leading.)

LINE WRAP Don't treat a wordprocessor like a typewriter.

Keep typing until the end of a paragraph and then make a 'carriage return'.

A self-publisher transcribing a lengthy court case (with copyright permission) faithfully followed the original line endings. His proof ran to many extra pages because each time he hit the 'enter' key it signified a new paragraph. This is a legitimate correction charge.

LITERAL/TYPO A wrongly keyed word or misprint. Resist calling it a spelling mistake, or ascribing it to the printer, especially if it originated in your disk.

LITHO see Offset Litho.

LOGO see Imprint/Logo.

LONG RUN A long print run of books can be 2000 or 20,000 or 200,000 depending upon the category and the market. Academic titles might sell in low quantities, a hyped novel might surpass the million mark.

For self-publishers a long run could be 1000. It is unlikely you will be able to push sales over 2000 unless you have a really desirable product.

LOWERCASE Letters in their small form, i.e. not capitalised. Expressed 'l/c'.

M

MACHINE PROOF A proof which can be seen while the job is on the machine (also called running proof). Last-minute colour checks and minor adjustments can be made but this facility is unlikely to be offered for short-run jobs.

MAILING LIST Collect as many names as possible to send information about your book. Buy demographic or trade lists, depending upon your subject matter. (See Database and Direct Selling.)

MAINSTREAM No harm in hoping you will hit the big time, but it happens to only a tiny percentage of published titles. Realistically the chances are very slim that it will happen to you, without financially backed marketing.

MAKE READY Preparation of machines before printing or binding.

MAKE-UP Text made into pages, traditionally from bromides in galley form, now being replaced by computer-generated page composition.

MARGIN The blank areas around text or pictures. It is very important to leave enough breathing space with good margins. Many desktop page-making systems do not allow this and you should modify their default text areas in relation to the page size you have chosen.

If you *have* to work to A5—although it is not an accepted book size—reduce the text area so the book can be trimmed to B format (198 x 128mm)—which *is* a book size. This could save some of the unforeseen problems that can arise at printing and binding.

If you are producing camera-ready copy in A4 for photo-reduction to A5, then be sure to allow generous margins and choose a typeface large enough to reduce well. Check your reduction is successful by making a photocopy first. It is always better to aim at B format rather than use A5.

MARKET RESEARCH Market research is seeking out books in the same category as yours (whether fiction or non-fiction) in bookshops and libraries. Is there room for another title? If there isn't, can you take a different approach? In bookshops check out cover design. Give more than a second look to covers that are striking in concept but economic in number of colours or special effects. If it means employing a designer who knows how to achieve similar results for a minimum production outlay, it will be worth his or her fee.

Market research is just as important for fiction as for non-fiction. It is particularly valuable for keeping abreast of changing styles in your chosen genre.

MARKETING Marketing is a crucial part of commercial self-publishing. It's no use treating it as an afterthought. It should be planned, budgeted for and initiated long before publication date. It starts with planning—including preparation and/or purchase of mailing lists—continues through well-timed advance information and media bookproofs for review, to author talks or signing sessions after publication. It also means cold calling, featuring in exhibitions and trying for subsidiary rights sales.

Learn as much as possible about your market and take every step to make sure it knows about you and your title. Knowing your non-fiction public is a good starting place. Make a comprehensive but selective media list for review copies. Even self-publishers of fiction can be well reviewed if targeting and timing are planned ahead. Enter competitions open to published work, except where self-published titles are specifically barred.

The cover is crucial packaging. Get it wrong and nobody is going to find out what goes on inside the book. Many booksellers won't purchase books with imprints they don't know, so be prepared for disappointments.

MARK UP Copy marked with information for the typesetter or printer. In professional publishing this is a skilled job requiring knowledge of typography, layout, style, and design.

Freelance copy editors expect £11–15 an hour. The very minimum you should present to your typesetter or printer is a style sample (a page or two from a book you like for instance). Indicate any subhead changes (Head1, Head2, etc.), rather than expect the typesetter to spot any slight difference in weight, position or spacing from your typewriter or desktop printer.

If you are doing mark-up or copy editing yourself, it is

important to keep to accepted marks and symbols. Any explanations must be terse and to the point. (See Author's Corrections.) Only copy submitted camera-ready will not require mark-up or design instructions, whether this be hard copy or PostScript print files. With camera-ready copy you get what you give—and you are unlikely to be given a proof.

MASK Indication of unwanted portions of an image. It is preferable to indicate how to crop these portions in soft pencil on the back of the original, than to make a physical mask over the face of the picture.

At proof stage, bold crossing out on the page is better than cutting and pasting so that the operator has to spend time working out exactly what changes you require.

MATERIAL Paper, board, etc. used for printing.

MATT/MAT Paper or board that has a dull finish, e.g. matt cartridge. Matt lamination is more expensive than gloss.

MEASURE Line length of text. This book has a measure of 23 picas or 98mm.

MECHANICAL Finished camera-ready copy, generally artwork.

MECHANICAL TINTS Tints laid down on film by hand to create tones of solid colours, where these are not computer-originated (see the green effect on the cover of this book). If you use overlapping tints take care that the screen is angled to prevent a 'moiré effect'. This mechanical process is being replaced by digital printing methods which are far more flexible.

MEDIA Send review copies well in advance of publication date. Prepare a one-page press release with a tempting 'angle' and relevant sales information. If you are lucky enough to be reviewed or interviewed, fax your advance

Anti-heroes in local writer's novel of a past Guernsey

by Fiona White

A WRITER'S best friend is a waste paper basket says Charles Wickins, a local resident who has just had his first novel published.

His book, The Land of The Donkey, is set in Guernsey and took about two years to complete.

He says that the story develops as he wrote and adds that even though one is confronted with the dilemma of a blank page the story will still gradually come to life.

The Isle was all lit up 30 years ago against a back drop of the growing industry. For Mr Wickins, who is originally from the East End of London, that period made the greatest impression on him — people were friendlier and the pace of life was less hurried, he says.

The Guernsey he describes in his book is essentially fictitious and he has reshaped the island in his mind, making it difficult for the reader to pinpoint the brief references to local places.

Characters are the core to the tale, although none of them make attractive heroes or heroines — "Mr Wickins says the "purely virtuous are dull."

His ... spend un drinking beads th being o the Guer way of th

Tom L is a craft with his out pay f He has a stamps a dodging t some of t

The co English Dickinson says that outsider's Carr, married a The owl house sil

Charles Wickins, the author of 'The Land of the Donkeys'. The cover was designed by his daughter Helen. (5175/2/93)

store a now from the UK. All but Dickinson were desirous of living in Guernsey — but none of them make an effort to learn.

Dickinson and Carr are called upon to investigate a petty theft which leads to the hint of tax dodges and the question of the existence of Le Page's wife. Helms's

his story is typical of any society of public body where lives or values or lines of money is mention.

Dickinson has a bitter sweet romance with a woman who enlists his help to find her sister who has married the right-fisted Le Page. They woman is the sort who is used to men falling in love with her.

Their brief association culminates with a kiss which falls short of the mounting passion Dickinson feels for her.

The sad romance Mr Wickins depicts depth life, he says. The itself is a rather sad affair.

Although he has lived here for many years, Mr Wickins says he feels like a foreigner here and every where. He does not intend to wish another story set in the island.

Reading The Book of Elysennar L. Page reminds him of how much an outsider he is, but he says he resents himself to the artist's lot to be a stranger wherever he is.

He hopes that he has written the book with detachment and affection, and fulfilled the writer's aim to entertain.

LAND OF THE DONKEY, by C.R. Wickins—Vincus Sanctorum, £7.95.

Ex-printer publishes his own story

THE STORY of the early days of a Wotton-under-Edge man will be in print before Christmas.

Mr Stanley Holden, of Parklands in the town, is publishing his book The Years Between, describing the four years before World War Two in Leigh, Lancashire, his schooldays and the depression years.

"They were shocking days," he said. "I think it is a story that is well worth telling. Family life as it was then was fantastic."

The book is dedicated to Mr Holden's friend Fred Fillion whose name appears on the war memorial at Chipping in Lancashire and only 100 copies are to be printed.

Mr Holden (76) joined the RAF in 1935 and came to Wotton with his wife Edna in 1946 after he was demobbed.

He then worked for nearly 30 years in the machine room of the Bailey Newspaper Group until his retirement aged 63.

He has been devoting most evenings for the past four years to working on the book and says his wife will be relieved that it is finished.

Although Mr Holden edited the book himself under the name Edman Publishing Ltd, he confessed: "I had to rely on Edna a lot to flog the dictionary to death, not being the world's greatest speller!"

● Mr Stan Holden with the manuscript for his forthcoming book The Years Between. (92/20/84)

Trowels and tribulations of a female bricklayer

Britain's first female bricklayer has traded her trowel for a typewriter.

In 1978, 60 year old Joyce Ward, from Standon near Eccleshall, bravely embarked on a City and Guilds course in brickwork.

Now, some 14 years later, she has published the story of how, despite working on a full-time course, looking after an ageing mother and bringing up four growing children single-handedly, she found the time to entertain what some saw as a silly idea.

Joyce has always been interested in bricks and brickwork and showed she was not a woman to give up easily by becoming a fully trained nurse at 30.

She said: "I wanted to prove to the sceptics that a woman could tackle a traditionally male-dominated area, but the main reason for taking up the course was to extend my increasingly crowded cottage home."

An Extraordinary Mix is a humorous and triumphant story.

Priced £6.99 paperback, £10.99 hardback, it's available from all local bookshops.

Picture by Trevor Roberts

Doctor's wife led a busy life

THE hectic life of a doctor's wife in Hackney is illustrated in a book written under the pseudonym Margie Fairchild.

The Doctor's Wife describes Marjorie Bielefsky's experience in Hackney in the 1940s and '50s when the surgery was their home and was open at all hours.

The book reveals how little spare was left for a private life - and how the friend-ly and forth-right personalities of East End patients compensated for the intensive.

Marjorie Bielefsky, who lived in Hack-ney for 10 years after the Second World War, is now in her 70s. The Doctor's Wife is due to be published by Speedwell Publications in the spring.

Living in Spain

□ RICHMOND author, Barbara Ambrose has this week published her first book, entitled Almeria to Aguilas.

Barbara Ambrose, the Richmond author and publisher of Almeria to Aguilas.

Barbara, who spends half her time living in Spain and half on Richmond Hill has written the collection of short articles which paints an 'inside story' of a more than ordinary view of the merged English, who live in Southern Spain.

The book reveals a personal appraisal of the pitfalls and pleasures to be found on the Costa Del Sol but in a way than can only be captured by someone living and breathing the Mediterranean country.

The book of nine short stories is unusually published by Ms Ambrose and is sold by the author herself. She decided to sell the book 'through word of mouth,' and anyone who would like to purchase Almeria to Aguilas should contact Barbara Ambrose at Almeria Press, 127 High Street, Teddington, it costs £4.50.

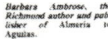

Self-publishers' press cuttings from Devon, Guernsey,
Stafford, Hackney and Teddington (London)

information, marked 'reader enquiry desk' or 'phone-in desk' to magazines, newspapers or TV and radio stations. They will be happy to pass enquiries direct to you to deal with, and will often mention your details in their columns or on air.

METAPHOR 'Never use a metaphor, simile or other figure of speech which you are used to seeing in print...There is a huge dump of worn out metaphors which are merely used because they save people the trouble of inventing phrases for themselves' (George Orwell, *Politics and the English Language* 1946). (See also Clichés.)

MICRON Thickness of stock, generally board. Board of 250 microns will be lighter than 250gsm board, so the latter is better for covering paperbacks.

MINUTIAE Ruthlessly cut all passages bogged down with too much detail.

MOCK-UP A planning rough which will help you decide spine width, extent, format, cover/jacket size, etc.

MOIRE EFFECT A wavy pattern that occurs when a screen is not angled correctly. You can see it sometimes when pictures previously published (like newspaper cuttings) are used as originals for a reprint.

MONOGRAPH Single-subject academic works are ideal for short-run digital printing. If they can be designed in a format that can be printed 'two-to-view' they will be inexpensive to produce.

MONTAGE Pictures brought together in a composite design. A very useful device in artwork preparation. Many large publishing houses are adopting it for computer-generated covers and jackets.

MORAL RIGHTS see Copyright.

N

NARRATOR VOICE Restrict that 'teller-of-the-tale' voice that so easily creeps into fiction. Let the story unfold before the reader's eyes as it happens, rather like actors staging a drama in an active rather than a storyteller voice.

NEGATIVE Screened negatives or positives required for offset litho printing. Ask your printer if film should be provided 'negative or positive, right or left reading, emulsion side down or up'. Film is more expensive than scanned bromides or PMTs. It can't be pasted onto camera-ready copy, but the result will be superior. (See Film.)

NETWORK PUBLISHING Land-based cable networks (like the Internet) can link author–publishers to end-users, bypassing traditional publishing and distributing processes. But the retention of copyright is a grey area—information could be used at will, plagiarised and altered.

NEWS RELEASE Keep press releases short (no more than one page including sales details—see Advance Information). Use few, or better no, adjectives and write in the third person. Find an angle to catch a busy newsdesk's attention—one that is genuinely newsworthy or linked to a current fad or event. One self-publisher linked (successfully) to an attempt to break the world speed record for book production. A media mailing company was engaged to deliver review copies hot off the press to reviewers. This was necessary to the 'angle' but you could also engage a company like PIMS UK Ltd (tel 0171 226 1000) to mail nationwide for you. With a good news release (there are many books on the subject in reference libraries) you can attract media attention. Self-publishers have led review pages in national newspapers. These days 'unknown' small publishers' imprints often belong to self-publishers.

Don't expect massive sales from your mailing. Reaction from the media can be surprisingly silent, even about titles from name publishers. Use press clippings to strengthen your approach to sales outlets. Mount and laminate them for local bookshops and libraries.

NON-FICTION Non-fiction still remains a publisher's best prospect—these writers often know their markets better than publishers or literary agents. There have been many non-fiction successes, notably *Nostradamus Understood* found in a library by a packager who fashioned it into a glossy coffee-table edition. Within four years it had sold over a million copies, and was translated into four languages.

NOVELS Nowadays, considering that publishers' first editions of new writers' work are printed in three- and not four-figure quantities, it is a less daunting prospect for novelists to contemplate publishing themselves. *Hack*, a self-financed crime novel, was bought within three months by a major publisher in a three-book deal set to make John Burns a 'name' we will hear in the future. Most published novels are not 'first' novels.

NUMBERS It looks better to spell out numbers below 100. Whatever you decide be consistent.

O

OFFPRINT Sections of a book printed for use elsewhere, e.g. a chapter or a few pages sent with advance information. Digital printing makes it easy for selective printing of sections from reference books, extracts from academic publications, etc. The originating author's copyright must be respected.

OFFSET LITHO Offset lithographic printing with rubber rollers transferring images on lithographic plates to paper or board. Digital printing is predicted to eclipse sheetfed litho in the near future.

OPAQUE Solid, non see-through. Used as a verb it means retouching negative film to delete certain portions. Useful for last-minute corrections.

OPTIMISM You have to have some optimism to publish at all. But don't set up an offshore company (it has been done) or make your run length tens of thousands of copies in your specification for estimates. 'My book should be in every religious library in the country' and 'I'd like to see my guide as the set book on the subject' would be over-optimistic.

OPTION A commitment to allow secondary rights to be considered within a specified time limit, often for an agreed fee. Options can be renewed—one literary novelist lives on film option renewals for her fantasy stories published by a well-known publisher not over-generous with royalties.

ORDERS These don't often happen unless you do the leg work to *make* them happen. Remember that it can take twenty minutes or more to service a single order, and this time should be reflected in your cover price.

ORIGINAL Text or pictures before any reproduction process has been applied.

ORIGINATION Processing all the work which is necessary to make your book look just as good if you have two hundred copies as if you opt for a thousand. Typesetting from disk, typescript, camera-ready copy, cover design and camera-ready artwork, negs or scans of illustrations are all forms of origination. It is very tempting to undertake the processes of origination yourself, especially if you have spent money on a sophisticated desktop publishing system. This might save cost but will it sell books? The least you should do is study reference books on design and typography.

If your job is camera-ready you will have taken care of

the origination. But the question always remains: have you followed time-honoured typographic conventions? (See also Typesetting.)

Origination costs are paid once and should be treated as an *investment*. The better the total package looks, the more chance it has to sell. Your public must feel an impact well before they read your words inside your book. This is why good design is so important.

ORPHANS A line of text (often incomplete) at the end of a page—for instance the first line of a new paragraph after a break in the text (like this book—for reasons of cost). Pages look much better if there are at least two lines of the new paragraph at the bottom of a page after a break.

OUTLINE see Synopsis.

OUT-OF-PRINT (O/P) The title is no longer on the market and it has been decided not to reprint it.

OUT-OF-STOCK (O/S) An enviable position for a small publisher. And a small publisher can reprint quickly—whereas a larger publisher might decide to remainder. In the latter case an author can self-publish a reprint (see Page Copyright).

OVERMATTER Text that runs over an allotted space. Professionals cut their words, deleting sentences, paragraphs and even pages to achieve an economic fit.

OVERPRINT Printing onto previously printed matter. Could be a good review you want to overprint on existing covers or jackets.

OVERS/UNDERS Variation in quantity delivered from that ordered. The standard condition of the printing industry is:
> Estimates are conditional upon plus or minus x per cent (usually 5–10 per cent), the variation to be charged or deducted (usually at the estimated run-on price).

OVER-WRITING Most first books are over-written. Your first draft will almost certainly contain too many words. Stringent cutting means not only fewer pages and therefore less production cost, but also more clarity and easier understanding. This applies to fiction and non-fiction.

OZALID A useful method of proofing offered by larger printers.

P

PACKAGER Organisation which assembles all parts of a (usually illustrated) book into a marketable whole, selling secondary (including translation) rights to build up a very long print run.

PAGE Single side of a leaf. Page is shortened to 'p'; pages to 'pp'.

PAGE COMPOSITION A very important part of print production. If you decide to do this for yourself for a number of titles, look further than the popular desktop packages available.

PAGE COMPOSITION SYSTEM The software package that will allow you to design a professional-looking book. Top-of-the-range systems like 3B2 are all-encompassing but expensive for one-off productions. If you are a Mac person you can try Quark Xpress or Pagemaker. If you are a PC person, Corel Ventura (professional extension) is ideal for books.

PAGE COPYRIGHT Published authors wishing to publish their copyright work, which is not going to be reprinted by the original publisher for any reason, must obtain page copyright permission from that publisher. They can then use the pages as camera-ready copy for printing their own edition (which will need a new ISBN and a revised imprint page). Copyright page charges can be as high as £3 per page but is generally negotiable, and could be nil if the self-published edition is not for 'making gain'.

If copyright page charges are very high, and you retain author rights, it might be cheaper to have the pages electronically scanned and set to your own typographical design.

PAGE NUMBERS Don't place these too large or too low on the page (or high if included in the running heads). They can make the finished product look unbalanced.

PAGINATION Numbering in a correct sequence. It is easiest for everyone if the printed page numbers tally with the actual page numbers. This is why it is a good idea to leave prelims unnumbered and start the body of the text at, for instance, page 9 as in this book. Don't number blank versos.

Always number hard copy throughout from page one to the end, even if you have numbered the actual copy in a different sequence. A book of short stories was published with a page in the wrong story. It had fallen out of the packet, and it was printed without a proof because it was presented camera-ready.

PANTONE MATCHING SYSTEM (PMS) A guide of many colour variations standardised by reference numbers.

PAPER Paper accounts for a high percentage of your production cost. If you are not familiar with paper stock, send printers a sample of paper you would like. A high density 'bookwove' paper can add a third as much again to the physical bulk of your book and give a perceived 'value for money' look, allowing you to raise your cover price. Art papers and coated papers will be more expensive and are often more difficult to bind successfully. Environmentally friendly papers are becoming cost effective but the cheapest will be those in the printer's standard range.

PAPERBACK If you are new to publishing it is a good idea

to start with a paperback edition. There are many advantages in bringing a smaller, cheaper, quicker product to market. (See Trade Paperback and Hardback.)

PAPERCASED Books with the front and back pictures forming the material covering the boards (like children's and cookery books). Papercasing is becoming much more common these days. Papercases can be printed SRA3 and, because it eliminates the need for foil-blocked casing cloth, it is the cheapest method of hardback binding.

Papercased books have been known to sell for self-publishers in categories like poetry and local history, as well as children's books.

PAPER GRAIN see Grain.

PARAGRAPHS Keep these fairly consistent in length and on the short side. Page-long paragraphs are intimidating. Paragraphs separated by line spaces are not good style and indicate amateur origination, however good the system.

PASTE-UP A term used in the days of cut-and-paste but still used for computer integration of text and pictures. Don't cut and paste proofs. Printers will have trouble trying to work out what you have done. Make clear written instructions on the pages instead (not in a letter or on a separate sheet of paper).

PERFECT To perfect (accent on second syllable) a book is to print it both sides of the paper in one pass. This is called duplexing in digital printing.

PERFECT BINDING Unsewn paperback binding (see Glue Binding).

PERIOD see Full Point.

PERMISSIONS You need to ask a writer, artist, photographer, publisher, or other owner, if you can quote or use their work (if it is still in copyright). There may be permission costs to bear. The Society of Authors and the Publishers' Association recommend basic minimum fees for quotation and anthology use of copyright material. If it is published material the writer wishes to quote, it is best to write to the publisher of the original edition (to their permissions department). The earlier the better.

Obtaining copyright permissions, illustrators' credits or quotation acknowledgements takes time and could hold up production because your printer refuses to print without them.

If you have made every effort to locate copyright owners without success, a disclaimer can sometimes be used:

> While every effort has been made to trace copyright holders and obtain permission, this has not been possible in all cases. Any omissions brought to our attention will be remedied in future editions.

PHOTOCOPY Photocopies are useful in planning a publication. Printed reproduction will be different from photocopied reproduction. You might be able to play around with exposures on a good photocopying machine but printers are more likely to use one overall exposure to deal with the varying quality of your pictures. This is understandable unless you discuss varying quality with them at quotation stage.

PHOTOGRAPHS Photographs selected by an untrained eye are often not suitable for reproduction (See Pictures.)

PICAS and POINTS Printer's units of measure, best identified on a printer's rule. A pica of 12pts is used as a (fixed) space, like an em. The width of an em space is dependent upon the font size used. There is a (fixed) em space between the headings and the first word in the text in this glossary, not two keystrokes. This keeps the distance constant.

PICTURE LIBRARIES A very useful archive of pictures and documents. The fee you pay includes copyright permission. Let them know your run-length: use of a picture could be as low as £75 for first-time short-run use.

Mary Evans Picture Library (tel 0181 318 0034) is excellent for historical subjects; Hulton Picture Co Ltd (tel 0171 266 2662) for more up-to-date and everyday subjects.

PICTURE PLANNING This is necessary when there are several pictures on a page. Pictures need to be scaled accurately, captioned and have adequate margin space allowed for. Plan by cut-and-paste, using a photocopier to check reductions/enlargements. If you want the printer to process your pictures be prepared for extra cost. In addition to reduction/enlargement instructions, label each picture with a corresponding identification in the text, e.g. 16A and 16B—two pictures required on page 16. Always keep originals in card-backed envelopes. Don't use paper clips and never staple. Don't write

A one-colour text-only cover brought to life with an illustration from Mary Evans Picture Library (kind permission of NVCT Publications)

on pictures (front or back) with ballpoint or felt tip pens. Ink can sometimes be removed successfully with milk or lemon juice, diluted so emulsion isn't lifted off the face of the picture.

PICTURE PROOFS Don't cut pictures and move them physically about the book to alter their position on a proof. Printers need to understand what has been done and an arrow indicating the page number of the new position is all that is required.

PICTURE RESEARCH A process often necessary for non-fiction books, including biography, when attention to detail and good visual skill are valuable. Professionals finding and collecting pictures from a clear brief should be paid at least £12 per hour. Creative research including copyright clearance will be around £15 an hour.

PICTURES see Illustrations.

PLAGIARISM It is unlikely anyone will take your work and pass it off as their own. It is a serious offence if it can be proved—when you should take professional advice.

PLANNING Adequate planning is necessary at all stages in bringing a title to market. You might need to change your dream concept into a smaller, more manageable product which you can process within your financial means, eliminate pictures which make a plate section of ten pages instead of eight, or bind in paperback instead of hardback.

PLATEMAKING This is the straight-jacket of offset printing. The point of no return. Virtually no corrections can be made at platemaking stage. If you visualise reprints in longer print runs, make sure your printer uses plates that will last (not paper or plastic plates). Widespread computer-to-plate is an exciting option for the future.

PLOT Work on yours to make it watertight. There are many

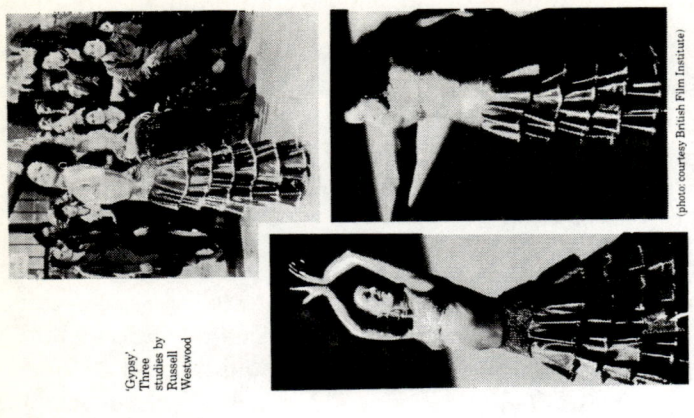

'Gypsy'. Three studies by Russell Westwood

(photo courtesy British Film Institute)

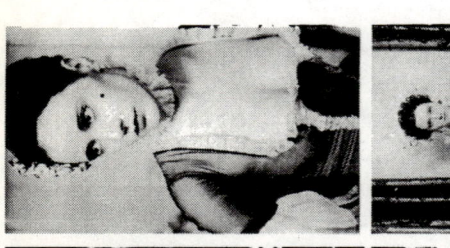

Above: With Desmond Jeans in 'The Blue Danube'. British and Dominions, 1931
Above right: Dorothy (Chili) Bouchier in 'The Blue Danube'. British and Dominions, 1931
Right: One of the beautiful costumes designed by Doris Zinkeison for 'Carnival'.

Picture planning is a skilled operation. A double page spread from Chili Bouchier's *Shooting Star* (Scriptmate Editions, London 1996)

92

first novels with weak plots, so yours should be convincing and well constructed. Don't include too many red herrings or characters, situations and events that have little to do with the main storyline.

PLR see Public Lending Right.

PMT Photo-mechanical reproduction of halftones. Being replaced by digital scans.

POETRY Poetry is ideal for short-run printing, not least because slim volumes break even more quickly than 300-pagers. Poetry should be very well designed, printed on good quality paper and have a stylish (not necessarily expensive) cover—one poet cut a dash with a black and silver foil cover, typography only. Coloured end papers can be effectively used in paperbacks as well as hardbacks.

POINT (pt) Typefaces are sized in points. If you want to save pages, choose Times 11pt instead of, say, Bookman 11pt.

POINT OF SALE (POS) The venues where your book is displayed, its web pages on the Internet, a catalogue or an advertisement for direct selling. A window display can be an excellent but brief POS. Display in a dumpbin is sought after but booksellers charge for the display space.

PORTRAIT Upright (normal) images on a page.

POSITIVE Film positives (possies) are used by some offset litho printers, as opposed to negatives. It is easier to make essential but minimal corrections on negatives.

POST & PACKING Send CRC, pictures and corrected proofs by recorded delivery or, at least, get a certificate of posting. Post and packing is a legitimate expense against tax. Offer 'post and packing free' as an incentive for direct sales.

POSTSCRIPT A page-description language that allows pages to be printed on any independent device that uses

PostScript. You could send PostScript print files of your book to Australia to be printed on a digital press, for instance. Watch out for the PDF development. This, in tangent with Internet marketing, will revolutionise book production in the future.

POSTSCRIPT PRINT FILES Saving your book to PostScript is within the capabilities of most up-to-date desktop and wordprocessing systems. Look for the facility under 'printing options'. Select 'print to file' and stipulate your floppy drive. You will get approx 60–80 pages on one 3½" double-density high-volume disk. Divide your book accordingly, always starting on a recto and ending on a verso. Remember to add blanks to make up a total multiple of four pages in extent.

As with printing direct from camera-ready copy, there may not be a chance to see a proof, although it is a wise precaution to choose a printer who offers proofs for your first book.

Ask the printer for their specification sheet and cooperate if they request that you remake your files.

PREFACE Author's reasons for writing the book. Keep it short. A preface is generally unnecessary in fiction.

PRELIMS These are the opening pages of a book and incorporate title, contents, foreword, preface and/or introduction, information on the publisher and date of publication. It is crucial to allow enough pages for the prelims (if space is tight the half title page and its verso can be eliminated before printing). The body of the book starts on a recto (right-hand) page. So the first prelims' page will be the first right-hand page in the book. It is usual—if space allows—to place the Contents and Foreword and/or Introduction on right-hand pages too. Bibliography, Appendix, Index, etc. should be similarly allowed for at the back, starting on recto pages. If space allows, each new chapter could start on a recto. Blank pages can be added at front and back of the book for 'even-working'.

The convention for the first four pages is as follows:
p1 = first right-hand page (recto), usually called the half title page, with just the title of the book (and sometimes a blurb about it)
p2 = first left-hand page (verso), blank or frontispiece picture
p3 = second recto page, the title page, should have the title, author's name, illustrator's name, the publisher's logo and year of publication
p4 = imprint page, always on the verso of the title page

On the imprint page you need to have a) publisher's name and address, edition and year published; b) copyright symbol ©, year and author's name; c) International Standard Book Number and British Library cataloguing-in-print data if used; d) printer's name and address; e) protective clause to save your work being reproduced by any means. (See the fourth page in this book). You should also include the right of paternity as introduced by The Copyright, Designs and Patents Act 1988 in the following words:

The Author's right to be identified as the author of the work has been asserted in accordance with the Copyright, Designs and Patents Act 1988.

A look through the books in your bookshelves will indicate the type of information that should appear on your imprint page and how it should be laid out (see also Prelims and Permissions). A prelims' verso page is also useful for recording *any* previous work of an author–publisher, however modest, so long as it is professionally published. It pays to show a track record.

PREPOSITIONS The correct use of simple words like 'at', 'in', 'of', 'from', 'with', 'to' can make a dramatic difference to a sentence. Inaccurate prepositions can change the meaning of a sentence.

PRESENT PARTICIPLE Make clear to whom or what a participle applies. Too many past participles—too many 'ing' words, particularly at the beginning of sentences—need to be watched. They invariably give a repetitive sing-song sound to the text. Try rephrasing in a more direct manner.

PRESS CUTTINGS see Media.

PRESS RELEASE see News Release.

PRINTERS There are many types of printer. Choose a book printer rather than your local jobbing printer. If the latter, or a copy shop, has installed a digital printing machine (such as a DocuTech) ask to see some sample books. Before approaching printers for estimates, you should have a clear idea of what you want your book to look like. But be prepared to discuss options and take advice.

When you have chosen your printer and your book has been abandoned at their door, your package will contain either a disk (or a number of disks), a sheaf of loose manuscript pages, or camera-ready copy. Your pictures will be enclosed in rigid card envelopes and clearly identified. There will be instructions and layout guides in a separate envelope. There will be no paperclips or staples separating chapters or attaching captions to pictures.

When the printer phones you with a query, you should communicate as briefly and clearly as possible, bearing in mind that your book is now in the care of people who don't know it as intimately as you do. Resist the temptation to send book-length correspondence. Some self-publishers have to have special lever arch files all to themselves instead of job bags. Others send handwritten faxes which are almost impossible to decipher. Printers hate information coming to them in dribs and drabs and you won't save any cost by trying to squeeze errors through by letter, fax or telephone. Wait for the proof.

PRINT RUN This is the magic figure that is so hard to get right. Household name publishers are constantly tripping over their optimum print run figures and this counts for a large percentage of the returns in the industry. The leading question is, how many copies for a first print run?

It is always best to have a short print run of 30–300 copies first, to get a feedback of the reaction to your book, and then go for a longer print run to start to make a profit. If Secker & Warburg print an average of 564 hardback novels by new authors, what chance do you have to do better if you are selling in the same market?

The biggest pitfall in publishing is the length of print run. An initial short run of 'taster copies', followed by repeat orders based on demand, is more sensible for self-publishers than a long print run with its tempting reduction in unit price. Nowadays large publishers seldom print more than 1000 copies of new authors' titles, and more printers are offering print runs as low as 300 copies. Digital printers are competitive for even lower runs, and reprints on-demand. You should have an idea of what a longer run will cost but do not give your printer too many options to quote for. Settle on a couple of alternatives and use these as a guide until you have the final specification tailored to your budget for a more detailed quote.

PRIZES see Competitions.

PROCESS In terms of full-colour printing there are four process ink colours: cyan, yellow, magenta and black.

PRODUCT Your book is a product. You need to research its market exactly like a manufacturer launching a new product line. Be very honest. Is there too much competition from a similar product? What has yours to offer that is special—your unique selling proposition (USP)? Can you price your product at a competitive level? Is it packaged in a buy-me manner? Does it have any perceived or added value? It could be marketed with an audio cassette, for instance, or with a magnifying card for the partially sighted.

PROFIT Many self-publishers make a profit but a large number are seduced by the ratio of falling unit print costs, the longer the print run. If your budget is tight, see if some ruthless pruning can reduce the number of pages. Must you include all those pictures? Large publishers give no sentimental priority to words or pictures—and neither should you, if you want to be professional. It is unlikely you will make a profit on a first small print run, unless your book is a slim volume in a specialist category of non-fiction which can carry a high cover price.

PROGRESSIVES A separate print of each colour to be used in the final job, useful as a colour guide.

PROLOGUE An introduction to a play or a literary work. Resist the temptation to write a prologue to contemporary thrillers. Often this is a flashback or flash forward and could have made chapter one of the book itself.

PROFORMA An invoice requiring payment before dispatch. This is one way to tempt booksellers to buy if they haven't opened an account with you. You might be asked for copies of proforma invoices to accompany export sales.

PROMOTION You *must* create demand for your title if it is to sell well. Trade publishers are promoting 'bestsellers' months before they hit the tills. Check if in-store promotion space requires payment. You can also submit your title for selection in trade promotions (contact Book Trust tel 0181 870 9055).

PRONOUNS Words used in place of nouns. Read paragraphs several times to see if you can improve on the placement of nouns and their pronouns—it can be difficult at times to understand who or what pronouns are referring to. Use 'its' in the possessive case, not 'it's'.

PROOF Proofs are working documents, yet they can be treated

a) as if they are camera-ready copy, with authors unable to defile their words by crossing them out. Correction marks are made with such faint marks that it takes twice as long for the operator to spot them. Or the offending ones are opaqued, then written over so neatly in fine black ballpoint that the position of the alteration is impossible to see—especially for punctuation changes.

or b) as if they are drafts off their wordprocessors, in which case they are covered with handwritten paragraphs, amendments and rewriting.

It's always best to be patient and wait for the proof to make zero-hour alterations. When your book is in its new medium, I can guarantee that anomalies and omissions will leap out at you from the printed page.

There are excellent proof copy mark sections in *The Writers Handbook* and *Writers' & Artists' Yearbook*.

Self-publishers seem to be under the delusion that their text is lovingly read by production teams at all stages, and that blind spots in their style are magically put right. In the days of typesetters this was more likely to be so, but nowadays it is better to get a professional, perhaps a schoolteacher friend, a librarian or, better still, a proofreader from the Society of Freelance Editors and Proofreaders (tel 0171 403 5141) to read your proof.

PROOF CORRECTIONS The most dedicated of book printers would find it impossible to keep track of every detail on the thousands and thousands of pages of text and all the job bags filled with pictures which pass through their hands, without sensible directives from each customer. Keep yours concise and to the point. (See Author's Corrections.)

PROOFREADING Whether page proofs come from the

printer or the typesetter, you should proofread meticulously. Better still, have someone else do it for you. Don't make any corrections unless they are unavoidable if you want the final invoice to look something like the estimate. Use accepted proof-correction marks and ensure that you use two different-coloured pens when checking your proofs: one to indicate the printer's errors and one to indicate your own errors or alterations. If you are correcting your own text, read from the bottom of the page and work upwards, so words are less familiar to you.

Contrary to what many authors would like to think, printers don't read the books they are producing. They cannot keep track of minute details on all the copy they deal with and your text might not have a human eye on it from start to finished proof. So the clearer your instructions to the printer, the more chance the final product will look like the one in your mind's eye.

PUBLIC Write your book for a specific public and it will be easier for you to target its sales.

PUBLICATION DATE Publication date is a crucial part of marketing. Time it wrong and you might just as well have not published at all. Ideally, make publication date three to four months after you can reasonably expect delivery of the first copies. Send out review copies, 'taster' copies to booksellers and library suppliers, copies for selling secondary rights. Then take a week's holiday from business or other commitments to devote to your launch. There is only a short window of opportunity on the wider world before your title will be relegated to a backlist.

PUBLICITY Publicity is often remembered only when your books are at last in your hands but are taking a long time to shift out of them. Hound your local media. Self-publishing is newsworthy so don't forget local radio chat programmes. The trade (including your distributor) is as interested in the promotional backing offered as in the title itself. They will want to-

Tip-off promotion. Chili Bouchier has a racing filly named after her by Lambourn breeder Douglas Marks (picture by Peter Bloodworth)

know if there is to be media coverage. and, at the simplest level, they will want copies and extra covers for window displays. If booksellers think the title is saleable they might ask for dumpbins. One self-publisher engaged a publicist from the film world for her romantic novel. The results were spectacular (but not cheap) and included a sales' deal with WH Smith.

PUBLIC LENDING RIGHT (PLR) Don't forget to register for PLR especially if copies have been ordered by libraries. Under the PLR system, payment is made from public funds to authors whose books are lent out from public libraries. You have to register by 30 June to be eligible for the annual payment in the following February (tel 01642 604699 to obtain application forms and other information).

PUBLISHERS Publishers as we know them came on the scene in the 19th century. They dominated publishing in the 20th century but their days may be numbered in the technological change heralding the new millennium. Demand printing and World Wide Web marketing might force them to alter their role, one that is equally open to self-publishers.

Broadly, there are three publishing areas: consumer book trade publishing (adult and children's in many categories); non-consumer book publishing—educational, reference, academic and journal publishing (broken down into STM: scientific, technical and medical); and mixed media, multimedia and network publishing.

PR see Publicity & Promotion, News Release.

Q

QUAD Denotes paper size four times bigger than a specified size, e.g. quad demy.

QUALITY You pay for what you get. But there is a general reduction in standards in professional publishing, making 'good enough' production acceptable in many categories in which talented self-publishers can compete. Don't expect coffee-table quality for a cost-effective short-run price. You get what you can pay for.

QUANTITY see Print Run.

QUARTER BINDING Binding with the spine material extending over the front and back boards for a quarter of their width (similarly half/three-quarter and full binding). There are taping machines emulating this sort of binding that you might be offered by some digital printers. Stick to conventional methods except for some non-fiction categories, such as comb- or wire-binding for technical manuals.

QUIRE A group of sheets of paper folded one within the next in a book printed by folded-sheet methods.

QUOTATION A firm price often given 'subject to sight of copy', when any changes will have to be agreed. (See Estimate.)

QUOTATION MARKS Make sure you know the conventions for correct placement of open and close quotes. Dialogue running in paragraphs has each paragraph opening with a quote mark, and a close quote only at the end of the last paragraph. Books in your bookshelf will be helpful. (See Double Quotes, Single Quotes.)

R

RAGGED RIGHT Copy set without right
justification—like this paragraph. End-of-line
hyphenation will give a tighter, more professional look
to text ranged left.

RANGE LEFT/RIGHT
       Line up with the extremities of other copy,
       either to the left or to the right. This paragraph
       is ranged left with the small caps above.

READER Readers are your public—write with them in mind, and never talk down to them. It is not necessary to explain information that is readily available in encyclopedias or dictionaries.

READERS (PUBLISHERS') Publishers employ readers to seek out any promising work from the 'slush pile' (the thousands of submissions received by a medium-sized publishing house in a year). If they have rejected your work there will always be a good reason for doing so, even if this is 'it is very good but won't sell in the mainstream'.

RECTO A right-hand page, numbered with an odd page number.

RECOMMENDED RETAIL PRICE (RRP) Now that the Net Book Agreement has gone, you can make your cover price 'rrp' if you decide to state it on your book.

REDUCE Make smaller. But don't say 'make smaller' to printers if you want them to think you are a professional.

REFERENCES References to passages in the text can be run as footnotes, or as separate sections at the end of chapters, or as an appendix.

REGISTER Registration of one colour to another in multi-colour printing, used as a noun and a verb.

REGISTER MARKS The correct printing term for DTP's 'crop marks'. The marks help the printer to lay one colour accurately on the previous one.

REJECTION Be honest with yourself if your title has had many rejections. Get some opinions—professional, not friends. It could be that you should limit your print run to an edition for family and friends.

A district librarian wrote to *The Bookseller*: 'I do not believe that there is a dearth of well-written books, especially novels, of interest to the general reader—simply that they are not being published.' Sent *Victor and Adua—Since We Were Four*, a self-published autobiography, he replied, 'It is certainly the kind of biographical story which would be gratefully appreciated by many readers of the mainstream of all ages, who are heartily sick of either the pseudo-literary or the semi-pornographic offerings provided by so many well-known names in publishing at present.' But it is a question of who is setting the yardstick for rejection.

REMAINDER Most titles on publishers' lists don't 'earn out'. When printed copies haven't translated into sales receipts, the edition is 'cancelled'. The author is offered copies that remain unsold (including any returns). An agreement can be signed to take over sales (see Page Copyright), but author–publishers have to try to find other markets, or cut their losses and destroy remainders. One author is insulating his loft with remainders.

REP Representatives who are the sales' journeymen of the book trade. Like typesetters their days seem to be numbered, but if you are self-publishing you will have to take on their role yourself. Together with typesetters and publishers' readers, they are the unsung heroes of the trade. Take a leaf from their book; make appointments to see bookstore managers and keep your sales pitch enthusiastic but brief and professional.

REPETITION Repetition should be hunted down and hounded out. Give your text to someone else to point out repeat opinions and other phrases. Run a search in your wordprocessor for words you tend to use repeatedly in speech. You will be surprised how often words like 'particularly', 'besides', 'very' and 'some' appear when they are unnecessary. Repetition in this book is for emphasis.

REPORTED SPEECH In fiction it is more dramatic to employ flashbacks rather than long passages of reported speech. When used, the first and ensuing paragraphs start with open quotes. There is only one close quote—at the end.

REPRINT For short print runs reprints are likely to cost as much as the first run of the same quantity. The unit cost comes down when the once-off price of origination is spread between all the print runs.

REPRO Copy or artwork that has been reproduced in camera-ready form (a bromide for instance).

REPRODUCTION Origination that has been through a mechanical process, e.g. proofing or printing.

RESEARCH When researching go back to source whenever

possible. It is surprising how easily inaccuracies can be perpetuated. For tricky subjects, or elusive pictures that will add value to your book, employ a professional.

RESOLUTION The quality of a printed image seen with the naked eye depends upon the number of dots or lines it has been broken down into in the mechanical process of reproduction. This 'resolution' could be '600, 1200 or 2400 dots per inch'. Digital printers are commonly 600dpi, but 'dot grain' on bookwove paper will often make text look more like 1200dpi. Pictures will have better definition at a higher resolution but there can be a higher origination price.

RETAILERS Some retailers (booksellers, libraries, etc.) buy direct from publishers, others will only deal with distributors or wholesalers. Try and find alternative markets, such as gift shops and district post offices for poetry and mind, body and spirit titles, delicatessens for cookery titles, play groups for children's books, information centres for local history. These outlets will usually agree to a 20–30 per cent discount.

RETOUCH Amendments to originals before printing. Many self-publishers expect miracles with, 'just write the motto on this (minute) badge a little clearer'…'add some lieutenant's pips'…'put in more cars in a sort of go-slow'. Retouching is a skilled art and does not come cheap.

RETURNS Don't despair, it's happening to the best publishers, with skip-loads pulped or remaindered. Check returns and send any shop-soiled copies back immediately. Don't accept any copies that a bookshop has asked you to sign for a book signing.

Booksellers and library suppliers should ask for permission, giving the reason why they wish to return copies. This could be that their customer has cancelled the order, disappointing when you have dispatched a copy with no delay.

You can negotiate with a reliable remainder company (which will offer very much less than the original retail price), but they are as selective in their purchasing as other areas of the trade. Expect 15–25p a copy for fiction, possibly as much as 90p a copy for good non-fiction in a popular category.

REVERSE Printer's term for mirror or 'flip' image. To reverse an image left to right is expressed 'rev l/r'. To reverse text out of a solid panel from normal setting is expressed 'rev b/w'—reverse black to white, even if a colour is involved. (A solid panel for reversed-out text is often indicated by a keyline only.)

REVIEWS Copies need to be sent out, allowing enough time for them to be read and reviewed (if you are lucky) to coincide with your publishing date. Magazines often have a lead time of three months and TV and radio programmes are scheduled well in advance. The media receive so many books for review that, if you don't give enough lead time before publishing date, you're likely to be ignored.

REWRITING see Draft.

RIGHTS Payment from rights' sales is generally shared between author and publisher, usually 60/40 respectively. Because you may be both author and publisher discuss a beneficial split with your tax adviser. Perhaps you could control some as author and others as publisher. Rights you can sell are large print rights; translation and other foreign rights; book club, serial and film, TV and radio and/or cassette rights.

RIVERS OF SPACE Lines are improved tremendously by close word-spacing. This makes the page appear as 'strips' of black alternating with 'strips' of white space. This is easier to read, but most desktop publishing has very loose setting with big gaps between words, and even letter spacing is employed. The parameters of most programs can be altered to give closely worded text with a good space between lines.

ROMAN Normal font style. A customer who wanted a quote for a 'book set in Roman Times' received a printing estimate set in Times. It transpired he wanted a price for editing his historical novel.

ROMAN NUMERALS/NUMBERS Use these as sparingly as possible to save your book having an old-fashioned look. It is best (if only for planning reasons) to leave prelim pages unnumbered and to start the body of the book at the next (arabic) number in the sequence. When you give your copy to the printer, don't forget to pencil the running order on the first unnumbered pages. It is out of date to express the year of publication in roman numerals.

ROUGH Work up several roughs for covers and picture planning before presenting a 'finished rough' to your printer or cover artist. This should be in proportion to the book format you have chosen and easy to understand. Be flexible—there may be mechanical restrictions that will affect the original idea.

ROUND-BACKED Hardbacks with spines that are curved, not flush. Round-backing is more expensive than straight-backing. (see Straight-Backed.)

RUBBER STAMP It is useful to have a rubber stamp (or labels) made with your publishing name and address, and your publisher's prefix when you know it (see ISBN).

RULE Single line on text or artwork. Also printer's term for a ruler.

RUNAROUND Text that follows the outline of a picture, inset copy, etc.

RUNNING HEAD Book title and chapter names appearing at the top of verso (left-hand) and recto (right-hand) pages, often with page numbers. Many page make-up systems can generate running heads automatically. Leave running heads off the first page of a chapter and blank versos, including page numbers.

RUN ON A mark-up or proof-correction instruction for text

to continue on the same line, not to be broken into a new paragraph or by a separate heading.

RUN-ONS AND REPRINTS Ask for these in 100s or 1000s in your specification for an estimate. The first is an extra quantity printed at the same time as the main print run. The second, printed at a later date, incurs machine make-ready cost all over again. With digital presses or printers using paper plates, this is very likely to be at the same rate as the initial quantity printed.

S

SAID In fiction you don't need to tag who said what every time anyone speaks. Check how dialogue runs from speaker to speaker in modern novels. Also check how dialogue is punctuated—most commonly: 'Phrase,' he said.

SALE OR RETURN Publishers are held to ransome by this stand on delivery taken by retailers in spite of cumbersome accounting and stock management. Try to negotiate firm sales.

SANS SERIF Fonts without serifs, e.g. Helvetica, Avant Garde.

SCALE To scale pictures to size: on a piece of paper draw a box the same size as the original. Rule a diagonal across this box and scale as shown opposite. Pencil an instruction for reduction/enlargement measure on the back of the original.

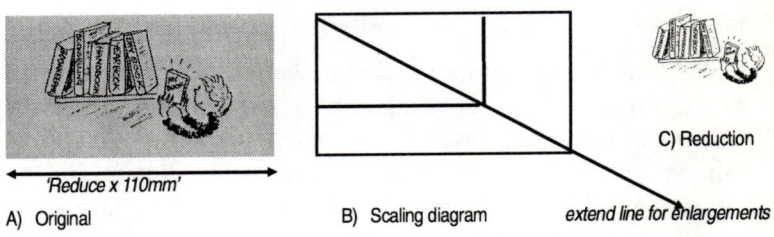

A) Original 'Reduce x 110mm'

B) Scaling diagram

C) Reduction

extend line for enlargements

SCAN Text, artwork, photographs, illustrations or transparencies digitised for use in a computer.

Few self-publishers will have the computer capacity to scan their pictures to a professional standard and integrate them into their text. Instead you can have your pictures scanned at a DTP bureau and saved on disk for a printer, or printed on bromide paper for you to paste onto your camera-ready pages.

SCREEN Number of dots to the square inch for reproducing halftones. Commonly between 60 and 130 screen depending upon the original, the printing process and the paper used.

SCREEN PROCESS A short-run printing process that is moving with the times and is worth investigating for covers. Look in Yellow Pages for screen process printers in your area. The screen is the silk or nylon used in the process.

SCRIPT A play is a script, italics can be script, but *manu*scripts these days should be *type*scripts.

'My book is in "Best",' said the author of a non-fiction book. 'Don't know that programme,' said the typesetter. 'Oh, best handwriting,' explained the author. These days there are few typesetters who will accept handwritten copy, so make sure your 'Best' is very clear.

SEARCH & REPLACE Use this option in your wordprocessor to correct dialogue punctuation or to hunt down words or phrases you have a habit of using too often.

SECONDARY RIGHTS see Rights.

SECTIONS Books printed by litho, web or gravure are constructed from large printed sheets gathered into folded sections. Folds are retained for sewn books, or they are trimmed off before glue-binding. In ready-collated digital printing no folding is necessary for glue-binding and it is easy to achieve sections for thread sewing. (See Sewn.)

SEE SAFE The purchaser is entitled to replacement titles if an order doesn't sell, or to receive credit. Better to make a firm sale if possible.

SELF-PUBLISHING Self-publishing is when an author pays a printer in the same way as a publishing house does. All the processes of publishing are taken on—editing, picture planning, design, production, marketing, publicity. If this is done by the same person, it must be supportable on a normal income, with or without profit from the venture. If you can't afford to lose everything you stake, don't self-publish.

SELLING This is the hardest part of publishing. It needs persistence and perseverance. The more leg work you can do the more mileage you will make. It means cold calling and letter writing, telephoning and mailing. If you can't sell, you should think carefully about self-publishing. Too many author–publishers think publication date is a magic moment when suddenly their book starts to sell. Look at a page of Whitaker's *Books in Print* weekly listing and you will see how 'lost' a title can be.

SENTENCE Keep sentences short and to the point.

SEQUEL Concentrate on one book at a time. Contemplate a sequel only if the first book is a good seller. If it isn't, do you really want to stay in the same mold? Wouldn't it be wiser to break away with something new, using your experience as a learning curve, dumping old drafts and starting afresh?

SERIF The small flourishes across the top and bottom of letters, e.g. this typeface New Century, or Times, Palatino, Bookman, etc., which have small decorative cross lines (see Sans Serif).

SET-OFF Ink that transfers from one sheet to the next in the printing process. French chalk is sometimes used to reduce the chance of set-off. Always flip through covers or jackets before sending them to the printer, to save 'spoils' being used in binding. Large areas of solid colour are prone to set-off—and blue seems to be the worst offender.

SEWN The most expensive binding—and still the best—is thread-sewn. But very strong slot binding is now available (also called notched or burst) for long print runs. Many hardbacks, especially novels, are glue-bound before the pages are cased-in. This is cheaper than sewing.

Digital presses are ideal for printing short runs of thread sewn books. No special programming is necessary. Just tell the printer to print the sections 'like individual booklets'.

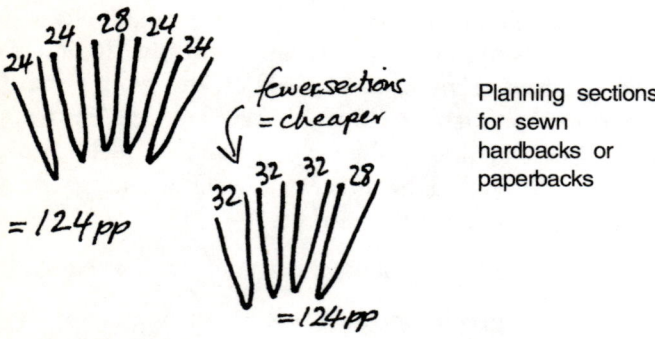

Planning sections for sewn hardbacks or paperbacks

You can work out your own sections and list them if submitting CRC, or break PostScript print files into the desired number of pages. Always start a file on a recto, even if the previous page is blank, and work to multiples of 16, 24 or 28 pages—32 pages if the paper isn't too thick.

SEX Don't include steamy passages because you think it will increase sales. 'Name' authors can get away with purple text, but you should tread more gently and leave it cleverly to the reader's imagination. A new fiction writer, feeling he didn't know enough about written sex, took notes while watching blue movies. His sex descriptions were original and alive. Resist using clinical names for male/female organs.

SHELF SPACE The slot at point-of-sale fought for by all publishers of new editions. This window of opportunity is restricted to a few weeks only and is made available at the discretion of bookstore managers. The greatest squeeze on space is the spring and autumn weeks because trade books will have been hyped for months in advance. Libraries too are possessive with shelf space. They like books that conform to correct book formats—any that don't fit standard shelves are piled horizontally.

SHELWING SERVICE Shelwing's mailing service (tel 01303 850501) stamps ISBN, price, number of pages, height in cm and publication date on the reverse of covers and jackets at no extra charge. (Always include these details in any mailing shot even if you send a book as well.) Shelwing also mails fliers which are very useful if they are good enough to compete with those from larger publishing houses.

SHORT RUN In small publishing terms up to 300 copies can be a short print run. Because books are so hard to sell in the open market, 500 copies can be a long print run. In more general terms, up to 2000 can be short, and long runs head from there upwards. A first short run will cost more per book (see Unit Cost), but it ensures less capital is tied up if the edition doesn't sell.

SHORT WORDS It is preferable to use short words instead of long words. They are usually Anglo Saxon in origin and have more punch than Latin-derived equivalents: 'let/permit', 'enough/sufficient', 'make/manufacture'.

SHOW THROUGH When the paper used has poor opacity, words or images on a verso page will be visible on its recto.

SIGNATURE see Sections.

SIGNING Book signings can be embarrassing even for well-published authors. Booksellers will order generously to

Two Scriptmate Editions' book signings. Above, Chili Bouchier at the Waterstones Harrods' launch of the paperback edition of *Shooting Star* when she was surprised by Michael Aspel for This Is Your Life. Note the blow-up of one of the pictures from the book. Below, Ann Kritzinger was given a solo signing on Mandela day at Dillons, Trafalgar Square. Note the display of *Echoes From The Land* covers on the pillar
(pictures by Michael Davies)

'stack-'em high' and many copies may be returned. But don't be put off—even self-publishers *can* do well at signings.

SIMPLEX Printed on one side of the paper (a term used by digital press manufacturers).

SINGLE QUOTES These are generally preferred for fiction and for emphasising words in non-fiction. (See also Double Quotes.)

SIZE see Format.

SLEEVE A useful marketing device. If you receive a good review after copies are bound or if you win a competition you can have attractive banners printed to carry the message to your public. The cheapest sleeves tuck round the cover like very narrow jackets.

SLIM VOLUME It is better to pare down to a well-produced slim volume, than bring out a poorly planned, insufficiently edited, longer work, which costs more to produce and will be harder to sell.

SMALL AD Cleverly worded small advertisements can be a useful way to publicise your book in newspapers, journals or trade magazines with a related subject.

SMALL CAPS It is good style to reduce the point size of words, phrases or initials that are capitalised.

SMART KEY Good wordprocessors and page make-up systems will have special keystrokes to give you correct em dashes, ellipses, fractions, etc. A common failing is a single open quote appearing as an apostrophe. Investigate the smart keys and you will find all sorts of useful short cuts to correct typography.

SOCIETY OF AUTHORS A trade union representing authors who have been commercially published in the UK, and a campaigning body for authors' rights. You can apply for full membership or associate membership and your published book will be considered by a committee (tel 0171 373 6642).

SOLID To achieve good solids on a cover might mean running the job on a faster machine or printing the colour twice. Digital presses have good opacity. Check through covers printed with solid backgrounds before sending them to be bound (see Ghosting and Set-off.)

SPACE Breathing space in design is good style. Leave blank verso pages wherever possible in the prelims, don't cram space at the end of chapters with pictures, allow generous drops for chapter heads. A blank leaf at beginning and at least one at the end looks good if even-working will allow.

SPECIFICATION Description of your book for a printer to give an estimation of the price to produce it. Here is a checklist:
- Number of copies
- number/size of pages
- how text will be submitted
- number and type of illustrations
- type of paper, type of binding
- type and size of covers/jackets (including number of colours)
- run-ons and reprints

SPELLCHECK Errors like 'Jesus went fourth' and 'Gabriella was on the urge of a breakdown' will not be picked up by an electronic spellchecker. General readers enjoy notifying authors of such misuse but, much worse, both these examples were exposed by reviewers. Always use a spellchecker to catch any stray literals.

SPINE Good spines are a must. It is unlikely your book will be displayed face out at point-of-sale for more than two weeks, if at all. Then it will join the other spines in a category shelf space, so design is important. Add 1–2mm to the spine measure to allow for cover board 'turn'.

Reduced colour separations for the two-colour printing of the cover of this book.
Note the bleed allowance extending from the trim marks

SPOILS Printing is a mechanical process and you should not get too upset if there are any substandard copies in your delivery from the printer or binder. Check through immediately and return them (or their title pages) to comply with the printers' standard conditions for returns.

Always make a generous print order to allow for spoils at finishing (see Glue Binding, Foiling, and Laminating).

SPONSORSHIP Charities are sometimes used as a means to attract sales. Make sure your percentage offer is realistic from their point of view and yours. This is difficult to achieve because they will need their percentage to be worth allowing you to use their name, and you will need to cover production costs first. A self-publisher who has sold thousands of copies of her six non-fiction titles can afford to give all proceeds to charity to celebrate her eightieth birthday. But a self-publishing novelist was in trouble when she based her donation on a print run of 1500 copies—nearly 1000 of which did not sell.

SPOT COLOUR Originate spot colours in solid black even if they are to be printed in bright blue or pink. Save to 'separation' in a desktop programme, not the actual colour you are after. Solids can have a tint overlay to lighten them all over, or in required areas (see cover of this book). You can have gold or silver printed in spot colour.

SQUARED UP Halftones, line illustrations, etc. which are aligned on all sides.

S/S Same size. Use the S/S instruction when pictures require no reduction or enlargement.

STANDING MATTER That which is kept for future reprints, e.g. film and/or plates in offset litho printing. (See Archiving, for digital printing).

STAPLING see Wire-stitching.

STATIONERY To be professional you will need letterheads and compliment slips. Include a logo of your imprint—and you could include the publisher prefix of your ISBN. (The publisher prefix for Scriptmate Editions is 0-9513766.)

STEP AND REPEAT A common imposition in printing.

STET 'Leave as it was' before a correction was made. Indicate 'stet' and mark a dotted line under the relevant words.

STITCHING see Wire Stitching.

STOCK/MATERIAL Unprinted paper or card for printing.

STORAGE Make sure you keep your books in a dry place, out of the sunlight. (See also Warehousing.)

STORYLINE The bones of your book, whether fiction or non-fiction. Think of it in terms of the picture visuals used to plan a TV feature—snap items that lead from one to the other, and each one important in achieving the whole. A well-constructed storyline should prevent you from rambling too far off the point.

STRAIGHTFORWARD TEXT Text requiring simple typesetting, like a novel.

STRUCTURE One of the most difficult areas of achieving good style is structure. This can apply as much to sentence construction as to the manner in which the whole book hangs together. Many writers fail in good structure—in fiction as well as in non-fiction.

STYLE Self-publishers often disregard finer points like consistency of style, or they deviate from typographical conventions. Your book has to compete with titles produced by skilled people in specialised departments in the wider publishing world. If you've never had a sentence published before, never experienced a sharp editorial pencil on your words, are you confident your book will stand alongside theirs?

Ask yourself some hard-hitting questions. Is your style up-to-date? Are you careful about consistency of style? Can it be better edited or researched? Have you double-checked those foreign language words? Was it proofread thoroughly enough?

As important is the question: are you a proficient copy editor? Is your final draft free of the punctuation anomalies that creep into writing of every description? Have you maintained consistency of style throughout, down to the detail of when not to use initial capital letters, or words instead of figures for numbers.

A self-publisher I know analysed a published autobiography he liked and honed down his own, draft after draft, until he achieved a very professional style. His book is angled to a certain market he has identified. It sells, not least because of all the preliminary work and preparation which has gone into it.

SUBHEAD Look through well-designed books to get ideas. One author of my acquaintance had subheads scaling down to sub-sub-sub-subheads. Apparently he had coded the difference in a varying number of spaces before the first words in relevant paragraphs in his Amstrad LocoScript files. With professional typesetting anything more than a single inter-word space is lost, so all these clues were removed and nobody knew which 'sub' a particular head was. The author's wife had to come to his rescue and marked up the copy with a simple plan based on entries in his contents page (see Headings).

SUBJECT see Category.

SUBSCRIPT Text positioned below a normal line.

SUBSCRIPTION Some categories of books lend themselves to the collection of sales' subscriptions before publication date, and this can be effected while waiting for delivery from your printer. Most of the major poets and authors of the classics subsidised their published work in some way. Chaucer's patron was John of Gaunt, Shakespeare's, the Earl of Southampton. Walter Scott and James Ballantyne published themselves anonymously. Commission, private or subscription publishing were widely accepted for centuries, and can successfully be employed today (see Dues).

SUBSIDIARY RIGHTS Selling subsidiary rights is the major contributory factor to profit for professional publishers. And subsidiary sales can be the surprise factor in self-publishing. Film and TV rights, cassette rights, translation rights, large print rights, have all been sold by self-publishers. A self-published novel exhibited on the Independent Publishers' Guild stand at the London International Book Fair attracted a German hardback translation option. An author sold large-print rights before publication date of a self-published fantasy novel. Talking book rights can be negotiated early in the publishing process.

SUBTITLE An important part of marketing. If your book has an apposite subtitle it can be easier to identify by librarians or browsers at bookshelves. It should have at least one keyword signalling its category. For instance, a book of World War I poetry with a romantic word for a title will sell better accompanied by a subtitle giving a significant date or event. Collectors could hit it on the Internet, or it could be found by organisers of commemorative events.

SUPERIMPOSE Check with your printer if you want images superimposed on other images. It may not always be possible to achieve exactly what you would like.

SUPERSCRIPT Text (usually figures or asterisks) that is raised above a normal line.

SURF Browse pages on World Wide Web sites. Look out

for sites which are featuring small publishers in their lists of titles for sale. The US is ahead of the UK in this field.

SWATCH A collection of colours, such as the Pantone range, that you can choose from at your printer.

SYNOPSIS A brief summary of your book. Ideally it should be short (not more than 1000 words), written in the present tense, and should reveal a *raison d'être* for non-fiction or a focus for fiction.

SYNTAX Correct arrangement of words in a sentence ensures clarity of meaning. (See Grammar.)

SYSTEMS Printers and typesetters can accommodate most computer systems these days. If there is something amiss it is unlikely to be your system in question, but your shortcomings as operator, designer, editor or typesetter. There is a wide range of good manuals, books, and information on the Internet, about systems of all types.

T

TAG Parameters given to paragraphs so that they will print in a particular style. Text can be tagged in your wordprocessor for speed and accuracy. Mark all changes to body copy style with symbols (such as \, #, ^, etc), then convert globally to the codes required by your page make-up system. Professional typesetters use this method.

TAKING DELIVERY When you receive your books, check the quantity on the delivery slip before you sign it. Traditionally there is a ten per cent leeway in copies delivered (overs or unders) which is charged or credited. Check also whether there are any copies you wish to return because of defects. If serious enough the printer will accept substandard returns. Send back these copies immediately (or tear off and mail the title pages if many copies are in question) to meet the printer/binder's return deadline (check the small print on the back of their estimate).

Don't take imperfections as a personal slight. Printing and binding are mechanical processes and each copy of your book isn't lovingly and individually handmade as it seems some self-publishers would like to believe. Be professional, not subjective, about it.

TARGET MARKETING Always target as widely as possible for the chance of a small positive reaction. If specific-interest booksellers, known specialist groups and educational groups are targeted by name, a 2 per cent typical response can be improved to 25 per cent with certain titles. Purchase or acquire membership lists from category-related societies, associations and clubs and give a special offer, be it only 'post & packing free'. The Business Database of Yellow Pages is a good way to hit numerous categories countrywide for a reasonable cost (see Direct Marketing).

TASTER COPIES Before you outlay the capital required for a first print run, it is worthwhile having a very short run of, say, 30–100 copies to use for marketing purposes. Send them for review with a targeted press release, to library suppliers and to booksellers stocking your category. There are useful books you can purchase listing booksellers by category. (See Book Proofs.)

TAX For tax purposes an author is considered as a person carrying on a profession. You can carry on a freelance business in your spare time if you are employed. You can be self-employed or unemployed. In all cases you should take advice regarding your tax position, whether you are making money from publishing, or losing it. (See Expenses.)

TELEORDERING A limited company which transmits orders from booksellers to publishers that are subcribers to the system. You might also receive orders via Tele-

Ordering by mail, particularly if your publishing name has been logged in by a bookseller.

TENSE Use the active tense in preference to the passive tense. The present tense should be used for a synopsis or blurb but should be used sparingly in fiction unless you are an experienced writer.

TEXT The words in a book.

TEXT AREA The area taken by the words on a page, minus margins, gutter, headers or footers.

THE END Using this phrase is old-fashioned and is best eliminated from your text.

THESAURUS Don't be cavalier about using a thesaurus. It can be a useful writing tool.

THIN SPACE A fixed space that is one-third of an em space.

THUMBNAIL A small illustration often set within the text.

TIMING When you are serious about going ahead with self-publishing, set a publication date and pencil it into your diary. Apply for your ISBN as soon as possible and log the date on your Whitaker book information form. The longer you can allow after you expect to have bound copies in your hands, the better chance you have for reviews, press coverage and media interviews—all of which are geared to publication dates. Library suppliers and distributors also require lead time to be as long as possible. Book lists (such as Whitaker's *Books in Print* whose information is also used by WH Smith for their *Bookfinder* CD-Rom database for their branches) are timed to publication date too and have advance-of-publication deadlines.

Devote maximum energy and dedication to the first few weeks after publication. You can't expect to walk into a bookshop and sell copies too far past your publication date and usually booksellers will not display new titles for more than a few weeks. Competition is fierce. To hit the Christmas market you need to be ready to roll by the preceding summer.

TINT A lighter version of a solid colour, often achieved by overlaying a film with a 5–95 per cent screen of dots or lines to create lighter or darker colours. A 60 per cent tint made the green on this book's cover (but see Moiré Effect).

TIP-IN Process of inserting pages at binding. Used for frontispiece pictures, maps and occasionally for replacement pages due to (costly) last minute corrections.

TITLE The name of your book. It is also the term used for an individual publication ('your title is selling well this year'). There is no copyright in titles.

TITLE PAGE Page featuring the title, author name, imprint and often the year of publication. If it names an illustrator and/or editor, they will be entitled to share public lending right payment with you. It is usually the third page in a book, and has more impact than the first (half-title) page. These pages used to be effectively decorated. Today simple

A title page designed by Katie Ward (kind permission of Rogar Press London)

but good typography is often substituted for more elaborate designs.

TITLE-PAGE VERSO The backing page of the title page (see Imprint Page).

TRADE DISCOUNT You, as publisher, set the trade discount. If purchasers don't agree you can negotiate. Try 35 per cent but be prepared for 50 per cent plus with bookselling chains. For single orders from booksellers, 30 per cent—or 25 per cent for specialist non-fiction titles—is recommended. Offer a bigger discount for a small direct order rather than accept sale or return.

TRADE PAPERBACK A first-edition papfrback is becoming popular, in place of the accustomed practice of launching a hardback and following it with a paperback version. Trade paperbacks are often good quality, in C format and a high cover price, compared with an A format mass market edition.

TRANNY Transparency/colour slide. Preferable to colour prints for most reproduction processes, but provide colour prints if printers ask for them. Colour negatives are seldom required.

TRANSLATION Try selling translation rights before you attempt doing this yourself. A self-publisher benefited from Latvian rights in a large print edition.

TRANSPOSE Change the position of letters, words, sentences or pictures, etc. If the syntax isn't correct a sentence may not 'work' correctly. Or you might want to swap two pieces of information. Try to achieve correct running order—and eliminate literals—at draft stage. It can be expensive later, although muddles leap at you more readily off a final proof.

TRAPPING When one colour is a solid with reversed-out lettering printed in another colour, the separation for the latter needs to be 'spread' so one colour overlaps slightly on the other, and no paper or board shows through. Many software packages do this automatically.

TRIM Finished size of a book.

TRIM MARKS Final trim marks are often used as register marks on covers. Make sure you alert the printer if there are any alterations to the book's dimensions. This can happen for reasons as simple as a spine measure change due to bulkier stock being used.

TUMBLER A book that has been bound with its cover upside down. Even the best bookbinders produce tumblers.

TWO-TO-VIEW Books printed 'two-up'. Digital printers should be able to print any size smaller than demy octavo (see Format) two-up. Tell them to use stock that is slightly larger than A4 to accommodate the extra measure of paper required. The machines can take it, but you might find the printer has to order paper that has been converted to a suitable size (222mm in width instead of A4's 210mm).

An example of two-to-view digital printing which is very cost-effective
The pages have been imposed to the outside edges

127

TYPESETTERS/COMPOSITORS Alas, this profession is disappearing from modern publishing. They were guardians of correct English usage and spelling. You might be able to find a well-disposed typographer or compositor in an advisory capacity for your text through a small ad in your local paper.

TYPESETTING You can get typesetting estimates with your typescript when it is still in draft form. But you would be foolish to give anything but the final polished version to a typesetter—the cost of subsequent corrections is very high. Electronic text scanning of typescript, or previously printed pages, saves time and cost at the beginning but later corrections have to be manually keyed in and are therefore chargeable at a higher rate than the original setting cost.

You can eliminate initial keying costs by submitting your data on disk. Present your text without justification, end-of-line hyphenation, underscoring, inset columns or bold and italic effects. These embellishments will undoubtedly have to be undone, so send marked-up hard copy (or a style sample) instead. An ASCII file is often preferred by larger typesetters—most word-processors have this formatting facility.

Let the typesetter know the make of your PC and wordprocessing software. If these are not IBM-compatible your disk may need to be converted, either by the typesetter or by a conversion bureau. With an early Amstrad this might add considerably to the cost because there will be a greater number of disks.

Don't become paranoid if some words or lines disappear or there are a few broken words. These corruptions are not inserted intentionally and typesetters will be happy to rectify them free unless your data generates many conversion anomalies. In this case they may ask you for another disk, but they are likely to charge for the second conversion as well as the first. Keep your text files as simple as possible and you will reduce the risk of conversion problems. It is helpful to give the typesetter a printout of at least a few representative pages of headings and tabular data as well as the disk.

Typesetting is very different from word-processing, so do not expect the proof to look like your computer printout. Inter-letter and inter-word spacing should be tighter and there should be no line breaks between paragraphs in the 'body copy'. Do you know about em dashes and ellipses?

If you decide to undertake this skilful task in your desktop system, it could save considerably on origination cost. But it could also introduce resistance to the purchase of your book in the general market place if you don't observe professional conventions.

TYPESCRIPT Well-typed pages can be submitted for typesetting even though typesetters and printers prefer text on disk. Proofs must be read carefully: operators and electronic scanning machines can make errors. These are unintentional and you shouldn't be too upset by them—they will be corrected at no charge.

U

UNDERLINE Underlining is used to indicate where italics are to appear in printed text. It is not a good typographical convention to have words actually underlined on the printed page.

UNIT COST Don't be tempted to tie up too much capital in a long print run merely to bring the cost of each copy down. A short print run of between 100 and 500 books will cost more per copy than 2000 books but there is more chance you will sell out the smaller edition. Don't calculate your cover price on a profit margin based on your first print run. Origination is a once-off cost and all print runs should bear some of this cost. Be prepared to lose on the first short print run. You are more likely to sell out a small first edition if you price it to the market and not an immediate profit margin.

UNZIP To undo a 'zipped' file so that it is no longer compressed (see Zip).

UPPERCASE Capital letters. Expressed: 'caps', 'u/c' or 'u/l'. The latter often indicates the use of an initial capital letter—'initial caps'.

V

VANITY PUBLISHING Self-publishing is often confused with vanity publishing but it is very different. The committee of the Advertising Standards Authority recommends a restrictive guideline in respect of the wording of advertisements, but this can mean that vanity publishers aren't so easy to spot. Many vanity publishers go bust which is surprising when they charge authors four times (and more) the actual cost of producing a book. You stand to lose all you contributed—and the books as well.

Vanity publishers make much of the marketing they will do, but marketing will be allocated very low-digit figures in *their* budget columns. When the production of your book is paid for by you, why should they spend anything on the most difficult part of the publishing process? Better to take the reins and self-publish.

VAT There is no VAT on book production. But if editing, typesetting and cover origination are not handled in-house by your printer, these processes will be subject to VAT.

VERB Don't use too many sentences without verbs—it often gives a staccato effect which can become irritating for the reader. Keep verbs active as far as possible, not passive.

VERBIAGE/VERBOSE Using more words than necessary. Being verbose is a common fault which can be addressed by cutting and redrafting, several times if necessary. Mainstream publishers prefer first novels to be 70–90,000 words in extent, because they are such a high risk. The less the extent, the less the production cost.

VERSO Left-hand page (backing a recto), numbered with even page numbers.

VERTICAL JUSTIFICATION Text that runs to the bottom of a page. This can cause 'widows and orphans'. Many programs can correct unsightly lines at the top of a page automatically but will often leave a line short at the bottom of the previous page. It is better to live with this when dealing with a long text, than manually adjusting lines on each page to make the line count exact. It is very unlikely your readers will count your lines.

VIGNETTE A picture with its background faded into nothing on the page.

VIRTUAL REALITY A computer-generated environment, increasingly used in electronic publishing.

VISUAL/SCAMP/ROUGH First stages of designing covers, picture pages, complicated text layout, etc.

W

WAREHOUSING Distributors make a warehousing charge and you should expect something in the order of £10 per 1000 copies per month.

A large print order can be a liability if it isn't moving. The unit price advantage of a long print run can be minimised, and a short print run, reprinted as required, will look the better option.

WASTE, PRINTING TO Paper is produced in different reel widths and/or converted to different sheet sizes. If your book's format is too large for an economic size it will be printed on another size, leaving blank paper as waste. Ensure that digital printers offer formats below demy octavo at an economic 'two-to-view' price. (See Format.)

WEB OFFSET A reel-fed process for printing long print runs, using continuous rolls of paper. Commonly used for very long print runs, but being introduced for digital presses and short runs.

WEB SITE An electronic page set up on the Internet by organisations or individuals with a unique address that can be accessed by anyone with a modem.

You can sell a book on a web site if you have a good product. It is a wonderful worldwide showcase for an ever-growing audience of forty million. Keep an eye open for the growing number of book sites in the ether and give them a hit to see their wares. To get your book on the Internet can cost over £300. If you 'go it alone' the problem is not setting up a page, but making punters aware of its existence.

WEIGHT Paper and board are identified by weight, in grammes or microns. An 80gsm bookwove with an 18 volume bulk is popular for general bookwork, 115gsm art paper for more expensive picture inserts, 135gsm cartridge makes good jackets (especially if they are to be laminated—as they should be), and covers using 200–240gsm (or 300 micron) board are suitable.

WHITAKER INFORMATION FORM When replying to your ISBN application, the ISBN Agency will send you useful information, together with a Whitaker Information Form.

Complete and return this as soon as you have the following information for your title—ISBN, price, publication

Whitaker's Books
in Print

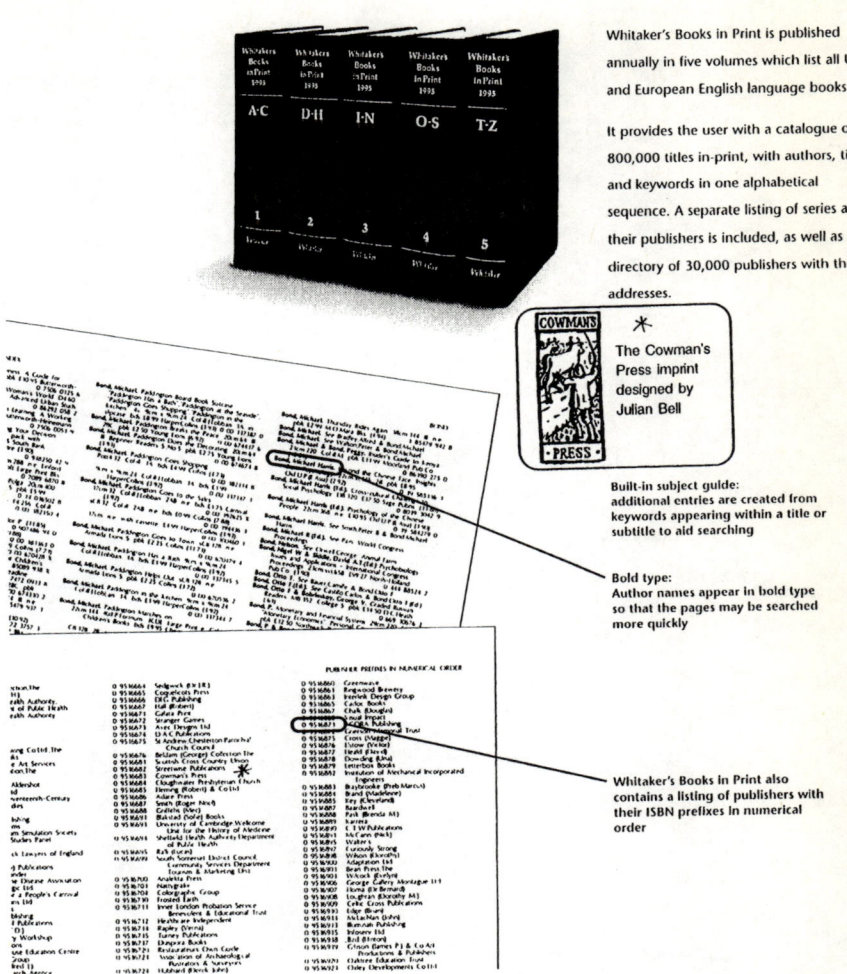

Whitaker's Books in Print is published annually in five volumes which list all UK and European English language books.

It provides the user with a catalogue of 800,000 titles in-print, with authors, titles and keywords in one alphabetical sequence. A separate listing of series and their publishers is included, as well as a directory of 30,000 publishers with their addresses.

The Cowman's Press imprint designed by Julian Bell

Built-in subject guide:
additional entries are created from keywords appearing within a title or subtitle to aid searching

Bold type:
Author names appear in bold type so that the pages may be searched more quickly

Whitaker's Books in Print also contains a listing of publishers with their ISBN prefixes in numerical order

It is likely that your title will be included in Whitaker database information (kind permission of J Whitaker & Sons Ltd). The inset publisher's imprint was designed for Cowman's Press by Julian Bell

Whitaker Information Form

Whitaker Bibliographic Services, 12 Dyott Street, London WC1A 1DF. T 0171 420 6000 F 0171 379 5469

Please complete all sections as fully as possible and return with any other useful, descriptive material where available.

Contact name in case of query			Date of publication		
Telephone number			Day	Month	Year
1 ISBN		2 Price £	3 Binding ☐ Cloth		☐ Audiocassette
ISBN		Price £	(✓) ☐ Paperback		☐ Other (specify)
4 Author(s) and date(s) of birth where known Surname first followed by other names			Editor(s), Reviser(s) or Audiocassette Reader(s) Surname first		
5 Translator(s) Surname first			Language from which translated		

6 Title

Sub-title

7 Height (in cms)	8 No of pages	No of volumes (if sold as a set)	9 No and type of illustrations	Running time in minutes for audiocassettes
10 Edition (✓) First ☐ New ☐ Reprint ☐ Revised ☐ Facsimile ☐			Name of Illustrator(s)	
Date of original edition		No of edition	Publisher of original edition	

11 Name of series & volume no	ISSN
12 Brief description of subject matter	13 Place of publication

Whitaker general classification

Children's reading key	Religious classification (if applicable)

If the book is Adult Fiction (✓)			14 Readership level (✓)		
☐ General	☐ Romance	☐ War	☐ Children	☐ Tertiary	☐ General
☐ Historical	☐ Science Fiction	☐ Western	☐ Primary	☐ Postgraduate	☐ Fiction
☐ Mystery (inc Crime)	☐ Short Stories		☐ Secondary	☐ Professional	

15 Imprint on title page

16 Name of publisher (and address if not a PA member)	17 Name and Address of distributor (if not the same as publisher)

18 Orders address if different from publisher/distributor address

date, author, title, publisher/distributor. These are the minimum details required for inclusion on the Whitaker database.

You should send the blue form to Whitaker Bibliographic Services as early as you can, ideally three months in advance of publication. This also allows time to send out copies for review and 'taster' copies (see Timing).

Any provisional details notified to Whitaker (such as price, extent or number of illustrations) can be changed later, but don't forget to inform Whitaker Bibliographic Services in writing as soon as changes occur. Established publishers are doing it and you can use Whitaker's blue postcards for this purpose. The white postcards are for any post-publication changes, or when the book goes out of print.

WHITE White, unlike black, is not a colour in print terms, unless white ink is used (this is possible with screen process printing, Indigo 1000, and embossing). If white is achieved by unprinted areas of paper or card, it is not charged for.

WHOLESALER A company that buys books in quantity from publishers and sells them to retailers.

WHOSE/WHO'S Distinguish between these words. 'Whose' is a possessive adjective (belonging to whom or which). 'Who's' is short for 'Who is'. An expensive blind spot for one academic writer.

WIDOW Words left at the top of a page. This is bad style if it is an incomplete line. Professional page composition systems have features to eliminate widow lines, but you might find previous pages run with one line fewer than normal (see page 65 '5'). This won't be noticed by your readers and is preferable to unsightly incomplete lines at the top of a page. If you are doing your own DTP and have no widow correction facility in your page composition system, add a few words in preceding paragraphs to bring a whole line over to the next page, or delete a few words to end the paragraph on the previous page.

WINDOW (GRAPHIC) A portion masked out on a picture or illustration.

WINDOW (SALES) The key viewing slot given by retailers to newly published titles—generally not longer than four weeks and often less than a week. It is timed to publication date and depends upon quality of advance information and cover/jacket design. The larger the marketing back-up, the easier it is to obtain display space.

WINDOW DISPLAY It is possible for small (and even self-) publishers to have their titles featured in retailers' window displays. (Ask booksellers if they would like a packet of covers/jackets and deliver them well in time.)

Study window display material. It is unlikely that booksellers will accept anything less than high quality (and therefore expensive) material, but it might give you some ideas. Like the small publisher who decorated a book display she managed to arrange in her local bank with laminated blow-ups of her press coverage. Or another who made a glitzy giant-sized 'book' cracker for a gift shop.

WIRE STITCHING Steer clear of wire stitching and spiral or thermal binding unless marketing computer books or technical manuals. These look unprofessional and the book or booklet has no spine, leaving no chance for booksellers to stock copies on their shelves. It is better to add more pages and have your slim volume perfect bound with a spine. Some binders can glue-bind as few as 16 pages (for booklets), so you need to shop around.

WORDPROCESSOR Let your typesetter know your software details when submitting text on disk (e.g. WordPerfect 5.1). Some programs will need to be converted, especially Amstrad LocoScript files (see Typesetting).

WORD COUNT When estimating the number of words on a page manually, count the characters (including spaces) across a typical line, multiply by the number of lines on the page.

To estimate the number of words in hard copy, multiply this figure by the number of pages. Err on the generous side to allow for heading drops and end-of-chapter spaces. The 'k' count in your wordprocessor is roughly the equivalent of the value of one character (usually found with the information that gives the date and time you last saved the file). Divide by 5 for fiction, 6 for literary work and 7 for academic work to get a rough estimate.

WORDS Keep them under control to improve your style and reduce printing cost. Delete most of those passages that you are especially fond of. Words are like jewels. Cut them skilfully and allow them to reveal themselves against a sharp setting.

WORD WRAP see Line Wrap.

WORLD WIDE WEB (WWW) The part of the Internet that allows access to pictures and information. (See Web Site.)

WRITERS Everyone who is literate thinks they can write professionally. Yet most people say 'I cannot draw a line', and they don't bring their work to public notice in a gallery. There is more to becoming an author than stringing words together. Writing is a skill that has to be acquired the hard way—by submitting to an editor's or sub's blue pencil for instance.

So much writing can be 'stream-of-consciousness'. It needs to be channelled and controlled.

WRONG FONT Use 'wf' to indicate where text has been set in the wrong typeface or point size.

X

X-HEIGHT The height of a font not counting ascenders or descenders, e.g. an 'x'. This typeface, 'New Century', has a larger x-height factor than the x-height of 'Times' in the same point size. Therefore more words fit on the page in Times. This saves printing cost but the text won't be as easily read

XEROX The DocuTech make of digital press is the most widely used by printers. But there are other makes such as Danka, Océ and IBM. All digital printers should be able to offer demy octavo format (or C format) in 'two-to-view' mode at half the cost of single A4 printing.

XMAS Three-quarters of all national sales are made for the Christmas market. To hit it you need to mail advance information during August.

Y

YELLOW One of the four process colours. Yellow makes an eye-catching, easy-to-print background colour for covers/jackets. It comes in a wonderful variety of shades.

YELLOWING Age will yellow paper unless it is acid-free. Store books away from daylight, especially if you have a long print run. They may be unsaleable if they are moving slowly.

YET An under-used but useful adverb. Sometimes it makes more sense than 'but', 'however', or 'so'.

Z

ZERO Check for any stray capital 'O's that have crept into your text in place of zeros, or vice versa. A good spellchecker should pick these up, as well as 'ells' used for ones, a common mistake for older writers used to working on typewriters, or when text is electronically scanned.

ZIP If your computer has a zip drive you can store 100 megabytes of data at a fraction of the cost of traditional storage media—the equivalent of over sixty 3½" high-density disks.

STEP-BY-STEP CHECKLIST

ONE	As much market research as possible.
TWO	Apply for your ISBN.
THREE	Decide the format and extent of your book. If applicable, select pictures to fit an economic page plan.
FOUR	Return Whitaker's blue form. Prepare a rough cover design and draft out blurb and biog.
FIVE	Send a specification for printing estimates to at least two book printers. Plan a publishing date at least 6–8 weeks after expected delivery from the printer; if possible, 3–4 months ahead.
SIX	Contact any cover artists, copy editors, picture researchers, indexers you wish to commission. Have briefing sessions.
SEVEN	Prepare advance information.
EIGHT	Choose a printer and finalise your text.
NINE	Finish artwork for the front cover/jacket and use it as part of your advance information or for a flier.
TEN	Cover to print.
ELEVEN	Mail out advance information sheets, covers and/or fliers.
TWELVE	Check first proof. Finalise index.
THIRTEEN	Prepare news release. Pass final proof.
FOURTEEN	Take delivery of advance copies (book proofs) and mail out (with news release) for review, approval from library suppliers, selected booksellers, etc. Make cold calls with advance copies.
FIFTEEN	Take main delivery. Send copies to the copyright libraries and fulfil early orders.
SIXTEEN	Publication date. Check that your book is in the system by ordering it from a few bookstores and a public library.

Further Reading
all available from Book Publishing Books, 45 East Hill, London SW18 2QZ (prices accurate at time of going to press)

Marketing in Publishing Patrick Forsyth & Robin Birn (Routledge 1997) £14.99 PB.

The Non-Designers Design Book Robin Williams (Peachpit Press Inc 1994) £14.99 PB.

Basic Editing Nicola Harris (BHTC 1991) the text: £27.50 PB. the exercises: £9.50 PB.

The Complete Plain Words Sir Ernest Gowers, revised by Sidney Greenbaum & Janet Whitcut (HMSO 1994) £7.75 HB.

Oxford Writers' Dictionary (Oxford University Press 1996) £6.99 PB.

The Oxford Colour Spelling Dictionary (Oxford University Press 1995) £6.99 PB.

The Oxford Compact English Dictionary (Oxford University Press 1995) £10.99 HB.

Oxford Thesaurus (Oxford University Press) £22.99 HB.

Rediscover Grammar David Crystal (Longman 1996) £7.99 PB.

Introduction To Printing Processes Michael Barnard (Blueprint 1991) £35.00 HB.

The New Designer's Handbook Alastair Campbell (Little, Brown & Co 1993) £10.99 HB.

Commissioning Illustration Martin Colyer (Phaidon Press 1990) £8.00 HB.

Looking Good In Print R Parker (Ventana Press 1993) £18.95 PB.

Editing for Desktop Publishing John Taylor & Shirley Heale (John Taylor Book Ventures 1992) £14.95 PB.

The Internet & World Wide Web Angus J Kennedy (Penguin 1996) £5.00 PB.

An Author's Guide to Publishing Michael Legat (Robert Hale) £7.50 PB.

Writers' & Artists' Yearbook 1997 (A&C Black 1997) £10.99 PB.

The Writer's Rights Michael Legat (A&C Black 1995) £8.99 PB.

Writing on Disk Jane Dorner (John Taylor Book Ventures 1992) £15.95 PB.

The Writer's Handbook Barry Turner (Macmillan 1997) £12.99 PB.

Writing Magazine (available bi-monthly from WH Smith) includes articles on self-publishing (tel 01667 454441, also for their bookclub list of useful books for writers).

Index

accounts 13–14, 21, 27, 52

advance information 14, 23, 45, 54, 73, 75, 78, 82–3, 107, 113, 124, 135, 138, 141

advertising 14, 16, 45, 93, 115

artist 18, 37, 59, 64, 88, 99, 108, 141, 144

author 9–10, 12, 14, 16, 18, 20, 22, 29, 32–4, 36–7, 40–1, 45, 48–50, 52–3, 57–8, 63–4, 69, 74–5, 78–9, 82–3, 85–7, 89, 94–5, 97, 99–101, 104, 107, 110–12, 115–16, 120–21, 123, 125, 130, 132, 137

bar code 21, 50, 72

binding 13–14, 22, 26, 29, 36, 54, 59–61, 70, 75, 77, 87–8, 91, 102, 110, 112, 116, 118, 123, 125, 127, 135–6

biog 14, 22–3, 37, 141

blurb 14, 23, 37, 95, 124, 141

board 23, 28–9, 32, 52, 58, 60–1, 79, 81, 84, 88, 102, 127, 132

bookseller 10–11, 20–2, 24–5, 29, 33, 45, 50, 52–4, 58, 68, 78, 93, 98, 100–1, 104, 106, 123–6, 136, 141

bookshop 23–5, 64, 67–8, 77, 83, 106, 124

budget 18, 24, 26–7, 36–8, 46, 51, 61, 78, 97–8, 130

camera-ready copy (crc) 11, 16–17, 28, 32, 38, 40, 51, 58, 77, 79, 82, 84–7, 94, 96, 99, 105, 110

captions 28, 90, 96

card 23, 28, 32, 44, 49, 61, 70, 90, 96, 98, 119, 135

cased 22, 29, 61–2, 88, 112

catalogue 26, 29, 93, 95

category 20, 24, 29, 31, 76–7, 98, 106, 117, 120–1, 123

colour 18, 21–2, 31–2, 34, 38, 43, 46, 49, 51, 53–4, 56, 58–9, 61, 67, 72–3, 76–7, 79, 87, 93, 97–8, 100, 104, 107, 112, 116–18, 122, 125–6, 135, 138, 143

copyright 11, 16, 18, 26, 31, 34–5, 52, 64, 66, 76, 82–3, 85–9, 91, 95, 104, 125, 141

corrections 16, 18, 20, 26, 35–6, 46, 50, 63, 79, 84, 91, 99–100, 108, 119, 125, 128, 135

cost 13–14, 17–18, 20, 22, 24, 26, 32, 34, 36–8, 41, 43, 45, 47–8, 50–4, 58, 60–1, 64, 66–7, 70, 73, 84–7, 89–90, 96–8, 102, 105, 109, 113, 115, 118, 123, 125, 128–131, 137–9

covers 11, 14, 17–18, 21–3, 25–9, 32–3, 36–8, 41–2, 46, 48–54, 56–8, 60–2, 64, 67, 70, 72–5, 77–9, 81–2, 84–5, 87–8, 93, 98, 101, 108, 110–11, 113, 115–16, 118, 126–7, 129–32, 136, 138 delivery 14, 40, 45, 68, 73, 93, 100, 118, 121–2, 135, 141

demand printing 10, 40, 97, 102

design 11, 13, 18, 21, 32, 34, 36–8, 40–2, 48–9, 51–2, 54, 59–61, 66, 72, 77–9, 81, 84–7, 93, 95, 111, 116, 120, 122, 126, 131, 136, 141, 143

desktop Publishing (dtp) 11, 18, 40–1, 46, 59–60, 77, 79, 84, 86, 94, 107, 118, 129, 144

digital printing 17, 21, 24, 32, 37, 40, 43–4, 51, 56, 60, 64, 72, 74, 79, 81, 83–4, 88, 93–4, 96–7, 102, 106, 109–10, 112, 115–16, 118, 127, 132, 138

discount 24, 27, 36, 43–5, 67, 106, 126

direct selling 14, 25, 36, 39, 43–4, 54, 70, 78, 82–3, 111, 113, 123–4, 138, 141

disk 20–1, 28, 33–4, 42, 44, 51, 53, 76, 84, 96, 110, 128–9, 136, 139, 144

distribution 26–7, 36, 45–6, 52, 66, 73, 82, 94, 100, 106, 124, 131–2

draft 23, 37, 45–6, 50, 70, 86, 99, 107, 120, 126, 128, 131, 141

editing 11, 16, 45, 47–8, 53, 59, 75, 78, 99, 107, 111, 119–120, 122, 125, 130, 137, 141, 143–4

errors 18, 20–1, 50, 63, 96, 100, 116, 129

estimates 17, 27, 36, 50–1, 70, 84–5, 96, 100, 102, 107, 109, 116, 123, 128, 135–7, 141

exhibitions 51–2, 78, 121, 137

extent 17, 27, 36, 38, 52, 64, 81, 131, 135, 141

fiction 11, 21–3, 25, 31, 42, 47, 53, 60, 70, 77–8, 82, 86, 94, 105–6, 109, 112, 115, 119, 122, 124, 137

flier 36, 54, 75, 113, 141

font 29, 41, 52, 56, 75, 89, 107, 137

format 13, 37–8, 41, 52, 57–8, 64, 77, 81, 108, 113, 115, 126–8, 132, 135, 138, 141

hardback 9–10, 22–3, 29, 48, 54, 61, 74, 88, 91, 93, 97, 108, 112, 121, 126

illustrations 17–18, 20, 28, 32–6, 46, 51, 53–4, 63–4, 84, 86, 89, 91, 95, 109, 116, 118, 124–5, 135–6, 143

imposition 18, 47–8, 53, 59, 64, 81, 128, 135

imprint 31–2, 34, 46, 64, 66–70, 76, 78, 83, 86, 95, 119, 125–6

internet 25, 43, 52, 67, 82, 93–4, 121–2, 132, 137, 144

ISBN 47–8, 54, 66–70, 74, 86, 108, 113, 119, 124, 132, 141

jackets 17, 22–3, 27, 37–8,

41, 46, 50–1, 53–4, 62, 70, 74–5, 81–2, 85, 87, 91, 112–13, 115–16, 132, 136, 138, 141

libraries 9, 11, 21–3, 25–6, 29, 34–5, 53–4, 58, 61, 68, 73–5, 77, 83–4, 90, 95, 99–101, 104, 106, 113, 123–4, 141
litho 21, 43, 74, 76, 82–4, 93, 110, 118

margin 11, 13, 36, 41, 56, 61, 77, 90, 124, 129–130
market research 9–11, 23–5, 27, 33, 36, 38, 40, 43–6, 58, 67–8, 73, 76–8, 83, 85–6, 88, 91, 94, 97–8, 100, 102, 104, 106, 111, 113, 115, 120–1, 123, 125–6, 129–130, 136, 138, 141, 143
media 14, 78–9, 82–3, 100–2, 107, 124, 139

news release 16, 35–6, 80, 82, 96, 102, 123, 141
non-fiction 11, 14, 21, 23, 25–6, 29, 44, 47, 63, 66, 70, 75, 77–8, 83, 86, 91, 98, 102, 106, 110, 115, 118–19, 122, 126
novels 9, 14, 16, 22, 25, 34, 42–3, 45, 52–3, 63, 70, 76, 83–4, 93, 97–8, 104, 107, 109, 112, 118–19, 121, 131–2

origination 11, 22, 26–8, 33, 73, 84–5, 105–6, 129–130

paper 17, 22, 25, 27, 31–2, 34–5, 38, 46, 49, 53, 58, 60–1, 64, 74, 79, 83, 87–8, 90–1, 93, 102–3, 106, 109–10, 112–13, 115–16, 119, 127–8, 132, 135, 138
paperback 10, 22, 38, 48–9, 53–4, 58, 60–2, 74–5, 81, 87–8, 91, 93, 126
photographs 26, 28, 49, 51, 61, 88–9, 109
picture libraries 11, 28, 34, 36–7, 43, 51, 59, 63, 73–4, 81, 84, 89–91, 96, 105, 131, 141
print run 9, 24, 26–7, 37–8, 43–4, 51–4, 60, 70, 76, 90–1, 93, 97–8, 102, 104–5, 109–10, 112–13, 118, 123, 129–30, 138
promotion 24, 26, 36, 38, 54, 98, 100, 102
proof 13, 16, 18, 20–1, 24, 26, 28, 31, 33, 36, 38, 46, 50, 53, 56, 59, 67, 76, 78–9, 87–8, 91, 93–4, 96, 99–100, 105, 108, 120, 126, 129, 141
publication date 9, 11, 14, 26, 29, 37, 45–6, 50, 54, 57, 73, 75, 78–9, 83, 89, 94–5, 100, 108, 111, 113, 120–1, 124–5, 135–6, 141
publicity 23, 100, 102, 111
publishers 9–10, 17–18, 20–4, 26, 29, 33–5, 38, 41, 44–7, 49–54, 56–9, 61–2, 64, 66, 68–9, 73–4, 76, 78, 82–6, 88–9, 94–9, 101–9, 111, 113, 118–123, 126, 130–1, 135–6

quotation, see estimate
quotation marks 17, 35, 41–2, 45, 57, 103, 105, 115

rep 25, 45, 104
reprint 17, 36, 43, 47–8, 52, 85–6, 91, 97, 105, 116, 118, 132
reviews 24, 36, 47–8, 53, 78–80, 82–3, 85, 100, 107, 115–16, 123–4, 135, 141
rights 10, 52, 64, 73, 78, 84, 86–7, 100, 107, 110, 115, 121, 126, 144

selling 9, 14, 23, 36, 46, 54, 67, 69, 77, 86, 93, 97, 100, 109, 111, 121, 125–6, 136
style 10, 20, 40, 42, 47–8, 51–3, 61–2, 66, 78, 99, 107, 116, 119–20, 122, 128, 135, 137

text 11, 13, 17–18, 21, 23, 25, 28, 33–6, 38–9, 41, 46–7, 49–53, 56, 59–60, 62–4, 66–7, 72–4, 77, 79, 84–5, 87–90, 96, 99–100, 103–10, 112, 119–22, 124, 128–9, 131, 136–8, 141, 143
timing 40, 78, 124, 135, 141
title 9–10, 13–14, 18, 20–5, 29, 32–4, 38, 41, 45, 47, 66–70, 73–8, 83, 85–6, 91, 94–5, 97, 100–1, 104, 106, 108, 110–11, 118–19, 121–3, 125–6, 136
typesetting 11, 13, 16, 18, 20, 26–7, 35, 40–2, 47, 51, 56, 58, 60, 62–3, 72, 74, 78, 84–5, 99, 104–5, 110, 120, 122, 128–130, 136

VAT 27, 67–8, 70, 130

Whitaker 14, 29, 45, 54, 68–9, 111, 124, 132–5 141
wordprocessor 29, 39–40, 42, 50, 56, 58, 63, 66, 72, 76, 94, 99, 105, 110, 115, 122, 128, 136–7
words 10–11, 13–14, 18, 22, 27, 29, 31, 33, 36–7, 39–43, 46–8, 50, 56–60, 62–3, 70, 72, 74, 76, 85–6, 89, 94–6, 98–100, 105, 107, 110, 113, 115, 119–22, 124, 126, 128–31, 135–7

First used in the *Daily Mirror* 1986

148